Just Shoot Me Now!

Autobiography of my "audacious" personal and work life showing anyone can maintain a sane career path and life if you try hard enough or drink mass quantities of Margarita-tas!

Dedication:

To all the truly compassionate women in bad relationships and hard-working Human Resources Professionals.

To co-workers and friends that impacted my life even some for a short time; Frank and Alison at the Tropics, Fran Johnson, Rebecca Kessler, Dan Klitgard, Ron and Joyce Noyes and especially Shawna Milatovich for the strength she has shown me to persevere.

A special dedication to my dear friends and professional peers Loretta Prybil, Suzette Murphy and to the greatest HR Lawyer of all time, Robert Klein.

Honorary Mention to two old farts, Robert Christel and Ellagene Diley who are the feistiest seniors I've had the pleasure of knowing and of course my girlfriend Steve Wilson-Huh?

To my husband Jim, my super stepdaughters Erica and Natasha and lastly to my beautiful and totally "Artsy" daughter Ginger.

Without them I would not have written this book.

Chapter I

Everything in this book is 90% real (unfortunately) and the rest is a tiny bit embellished in order to set the ambiance of the situation. Doesn't that sound aromatic?
Let's make this even more fun by starting the whole damn thing right from the get go with my personal and professional life as that has impacted my life's path greatly. Why not? Boring? No honker way folks!

Okay then……Let's dig in right away…..oh, I have to tell you right off the bat about some juicy happenings. This will relate to a lot of gals out there!

Interviews!

Where shall I start? The beginnings. Now most people don't want to hear of someone's petty personal life or the jobs they've held. Most think it would be too boring to write about until after I would share my past to my friends for the past 20 years. They kept saying, "You just have to write about this stuff." So………with that……

Let's start with some of my

Ah-h-h interviews. So many types and kinds out there. Standard ones, behavioral, weighted. I can't stand weighted as they pick their candidates through a scoring system and not truly learning about their skills and history. I'll tell you more about that one later on too.

Now periodically I will start referring to a loaded gun which is the title of my book. Some...oh hell, a lot of my context is so bazaar that I start with getting the gun out, and slowly loading the damn thing and you will understand why by the time we are done.

Okay back to the start with interviews:

Remember when you had a question on your electric or credit card bill? How many times did you have to hit a button before you even talked with a "live" person? Maybe you never did? That is a lot like many human resource departments. Emails back and forth. No one talks anymore.

I actually went through an extremely intense first, second and third interview all via email for a Human Resources Director position! That's right only conversed through email. This was a great opportunity to work for a nonprofit entity that helped troubled teens. I wanted it badly as I love helping recruit people that help each other in the community.

I applied for the job and waited. Dang if I didn't hear back right away. Yeah! I decided to do a little homework and research this facility so I can come across somewhat half intelligent.

Their website focused on their compassionate staff, personable, results oriented with success stories and so on. It was a well-established and reputable facility that's been around for years. Somehow going through the interview process it will be evident that they lost the "personable" part somewhere along the way.

But the first phase didn't strike me as odd at all. Most preliminary interviews are answering questions via email or through a phone screen interview. Okay, no big deal there.

Mine was through the email. Now these emails were personally from the Executive Director of the facility so I was quite impressed by that.

For the first interview round I had to answer some complex questions about what I thought a good human resources person should be. There were various paragraph scenario situations and I felt I answered them quite well.

They were tough questions and took me over an hour to finish. Then I sent it back to them and thanked them for the opportunity to participate (pretty darn good aren't I).

About a week later I received an email from the Executive Director and this time personally "congratulating" me and telling me that I had passed the first round. Now he wanted me to move onto the second round.

Oh Boy! How exciting. (Sigh). Here is where it starts to get shaky. He emailed me back and I was asked to answer 23 questions in 300 words or less. I despise these types of restrictions.

Man was that ever hard! I had all kinds of scenarios from supplying samples of human resources benchmarks, dashboards, analyses, strategic plans and chart statistics. To handling discrepancies between the President and Vice President and so much more.

This was very intense with intellectual questions that took me 6 days to complete (they allowed you two weeks to finish it). Well I had to work all day, then do housework so the only time I could finish was after work or on the weekend.

Exhaustingly I sent it back and about another week later I was once again emailed by the Executive Director and "congratulated" (Bigger sigh).

This Executive Director asked me (remember now - via email) to go into the final phase which was on what I knew about their company in depth and how I could contribute. That had to be 3,000 words, no more.

Geez Louise! I spent the following weekend finishing the final process and sent it in. I waited about two weeks, didn't hear anything and shortly after received yet another email from him once again "congratulating" me folks. (Sorry, I'm out of sighs by now). I made it to the pre-final phase.

Then he emailed me requesting I drive to their facility and speak to someone in human resources (not the final interview) for about a half hour. Not speak to the Director but a screener.

Oh Heck No! HALF an HOUR?! That's it? I just spent over 4 weeks responding to all your tests and emails, passed them all and I only get a half hour live interview? Hellooooo, anyone out there?! What can you really know about anyone in just a half hour?

Plus this was over an hour drive from my current location. I was so mad after all that time and effort that they felt this was the next step?

Seriously! At that point after all that work I actually decided to decline going to the interview. Yes, I know...maybe that was frivolous of me but to tell you the truth as I was doing all the requested projects, a lot of the questions and basically this whole interview process started to turn me off of the job.

It was slowly becoming not such an exciting opportunity after all. Now think about it.....I mean...if this is how they process me in an interview, then this is how I would have to do it to other candidates I consider for this place and that's just not my style.

Where was all that stuff about how compassionate, personable and successful they were? How can that be with the way they do interviews? What type of HR person are they looking for? Certainly not one who goes out of their way with an employee.

I emailed the Director and told him I was rescinding my interest. Immediately the Director emailed me asking why. Okay for one thing he emailed me asking why. Why didn't he pick up a phone? Hello-o-o.

Not one live conversation in this whole deal. So I wrote him back (**in less than 300 words**) explaining what went wrong. And specifically pointed out that not one person spoke to me nor did anyone sell me on the company at all. All the questions focused on my abilities but interviews are two-fold. I get you interested in me and you peak my interest to want to work there.

I stated it was the way the whole procedure seemed insensitive and made me feel cold, not a valued candidate. I was like a can of beans rolling down a conveyor line passing through several inspections and stamped for the next shipment. There was no human factor in this whole process.

It was okay for the first couple of preliminary requests but totally turned me off in the final round as I expected I had **earned** the hurdle of talking to a person.

I explained to him that in future I recommend a more personal way of communicating which coincided with their vision statement. Funny I just can't grasp this company helping troubled teens get back on track as they were sorely lacking any humanistic interviewing techniques.

It was totally calculated and decided on by statistical data. I never did get a response back over my comments. So there yah go…..

On a positive note, I saved all my work during this interview as I was proud that I made it "almost all the way." And maybe I can use some of the material in a future interview. So it wasn't a total waste of time. I can always find a positive because I'm a total optimist.

After another Margarita-ta-ta….Onto another….

I recall another interview for a human resources supervisory opening I had about 13 years ago. It was a panel interview of 11 female human resources representatives.

ALL from different human resources sectors within the same company. There had to be 8 of them as human resource supervisors from different levels of the same department in one building.

Here's a perfect example of my previous discussion on what a cluster of leaders are. How many people does it take to change a light bulb? Are you getting my drift?

How many HR people are needed in an HR department? How big was this company? Well it wasn't that big, the building was one story and about 50,000 square feet. Corporate was out of State so this was a satellite facility.

I sat down at the end of a table that seemed miles long and you could just feel a chill in the air. A very stiff and cold environment.

I noticed there was an obvious competition amongst each supervisor in that room. They all sat perfectly straight with their chests straight out, nose and necks high in the sky. No one smiled and they all had their pre-prepared questions for me in front of them.

Maybe they were competing with each other's questions? It definitely was a "who was better than who" or "who was higher on the command chain than who" atmosphere. Could someone please start looking for that gun?

No one offered me a coffee or water. Not even a "Hello" or "Thank you for coming in today." I was greeted with cold introductions of each person and what their specific role was.

Now these introductions were about 3 minutes each so with 11 there, I just went through 33 minutes of "There's no way I'm going to remember all your names and titles or what your role is."

And let me tell you something each had to accentuate their title with the company. "I'm Sara Hightower, the Assistant Sub Supervisor of Sub HR supervisors for the sub benefits area." Whew! Take a deep breath on that one!

This was a long title, but some titles were ridiculously longer. I knew immediately that this wasn't a place I wanted to work for. And so the tone was set...ta-dumb, ta-dumb, ta-dumb.

So knowing that this wasn't going to work out, I decided to make the most of it for me alone. I must say looked downright dapper in my new suit and hair up in a professional do.

I sat straight, looked each in the eye, smiled often and professionally answered all of their questions. I must say I was quite impressed with my answers. Many of the questions went on and on how I would act in certain situations.

Ah-h-h behavioral questions, my favorite! Some of those can actually be a good part of figuring out if you will be a strong candidate or not or you are a great faker.

By now we had been interviewing over an hour and a half and my cheeks started to hurt from all the forced smiling. (Where's that gun???). A majority of the questions were redundant as you can only create so many behavioral questions and end up with similar scenarios.

It was hard to respond with the same answer and change it up with a different flair. This seemed to go on forever. As it was getting towards the end of the interview, one of the **VERY LAST** questions was perfect for my ending and I mean PERFECT FOLKS!

It's a simple question....ready? **They asked me of my experience with diversification.** (A moment of space here to fully grasp this question). Now most of you know what this is centering on but I took it just a step further. (More space here to reflect...are you reflecting?)

I was done contemplating and decided to take this as an opportunity to cut through the chase and delightfully and loudly stated, are you ready? Here it comes….. *"Well I feel I have excellent experience with diversity since I've been married three times."* **Ohhhhhh Boyyyyy!**

(Load the gun as it's over now folks)

THERE WAS DEAD SILENCE….You could hear a pin drop!

All eyes and mouths were wide open and on me like an iceberg. You thought it was a cold environment before. Now it's frigid. B-r-r-r-r. I knew then and there that I had accomplished what I intended to with that answer and I simply folded my hands together, leaned back in my chair and smiled from ear to ear.

That was an excellent ending to an awful panel interview. Oh-Oh…but wait…one of the interviewing supervisors chuckled when I said that and all the others immediately turned their heads to her.

You could feel the wind shift as that's how fast they turned their head. Swoosh! I think I even saw their papers flip up from the wind of movement………No seriously.

You could see the knives go deep into the cores of her eyes....ugh. I felt so bad for that gal..no, not really. That was it! They had no more questions for me. Not even a thank you for your time? WTF? Right away after we departed I did a little jig dance while walking out of there. I was so happy to be done with that. **_What a crock of crap!_**

But I'm getting off kilter and need to get back to the beginnings. It was a nice start though wasn't it?

And last but not least an interview I just had a few years back. It was for a Director of Human Resources. I first had a phone interview with the office assistant and payroll person. They had their pre-set questions ready. I aced them all very nicely. That payroll person was something else.

Towards the end he stated, "Now this is the type of person I want working for me, I mean with me." Oops. Read between the lines, this person is controlling and possessive of his job. Oh boy! Anyway, I must have done a good job as then the CEO called me to schedule an interview with him.

Now remember back where I stated that I didn't like weighted interviews? That's what this was. He sat down with me and placed a piece of paper in front of him. He actually showed it to me. It looked like a review form with a scoring chart on it to weigh my answers. He was an accountant so whether I did well or not, it was all about the final score.

He would ask his questions about my past and abilities. I did very well at the end. The next phase would be to meet all the other executives in the final interview process. He said he would call me whether I made it that far or not. Well he called a few days later and said he was considering two others because their current job titles had the word "Director" on it.

WHAT?!

I explained to him that my last three jobs had "Director" titles on them. Just because my current job is a "Manager" title that disqualified me? He even said I answered a lot of the questions better but it's all about that title folks. What a crock of crap! Where's that poop again?!

That was so bogus. Well I certainly hope it works out for them. I was getting turned off by the interview process anyway. I'm old school and when I interview I take a lot more into consideration.

My gut feelings, their background in depth, personality and accomplishments. Not what the score or psychological test says. That's like online dating. You're really not going to know that person from data input. You know I've said this more than once in an interview.

Whenever they ask me why we should hire you over another qualified candidate I look at them and say, "Look, it's a 50/50 chance I'm going to be the person or anyone else right for this job." That's always the way it is in any retention effort. You hope it all works out.

They look at me so different when I make that candid statement. But it's gotten me a lot of opportunities because they want someone who is working in reality and not sugar coat it.

Chapter II

Okay, enough start with the interviews I've had. We'll have more later on that are funny. Now real beginning.

Back in 1972 after high school graduation unknown to me at the time my parents enrolled me into an airline school out of State. I found out when a representative stopped by our house one night in a Karman Ghia car. Remember those?

By the time they told me about it I only had a week off between high school graduation and starting this school. How nice.

I had a boyfriend I had to say good-bye to and tons of friends from school. I was very popular in school, was in drama class and a cheerleader.

I had a part-time job so needed to put in notice right away. There was no time to relax, had to pack and get my head in the right place for this. Not that I didn't want to do it, but I would have liked to have been at the meeting and absorb the contemplation first. Dang!

It was so soon, so fast. I was scared and excited all at once as this would be the first time I was leaving the home nest which was actually good as I would be 18 in a few months. My family life was very dysfunctional. But who's wasn't in some form?

I have to say it had to be very difficult for my parents to raise seven kids by the time they were 32 years old. All about two years apart from each other. It was dysfunctional by necessity.

There's an awful lot that happened in our childhood that affected most of our life outcomes, but that's another book someday. Getting back to the subject matter at hand.............

Mom and dad drove me a few States out to this school. When I got there I found out I was to share a room in with two other classmates in an old hotel that was set up dormitory style. More exciting news! Sleeping with complete strangers! **Yippee!**

Man, how uncomfortable. Not only just finishing high school, leaving home, leaving my friends, leaving my boyfriend, but living with strangers just like that?

Either accept it or go back and going back was NOT AN OPTION! As we were moving in my shared room and getting set up for airline school soon the two other gals started moving in at the same time.

Believe it or not, all our first names were identical and spelled the same (such luck).

We were all totally different in personality though and never became really close friends. One was a wild party animal and the other the shy domestic type that was a wannabe party girl (she ended up getting pregnant during school by the way). How the heck does that happen? Really?

The schooling was eight hours per day and five days per week for three solid months. It was a pretty rigorous course with teachers who expected results. I concentrated on my classes very diligently as I dreamed of becoming a stewardess one day. "Coffee, tea or me anyone?" Gosh that's so old!

My other two roommates had a different agenda of partying every night and finding boyfriends. It was very difficult to get your homework done or study with guys and gals walking in and out of your apartment all the time. Some stayed all night and played loud music or left the television on full blast.

It was very distracting and nerve racking. You had to go through our bedroom to get to the bathroom. There was literally no privacy AT ALL! After about a month of that torture I was fortunate to take on a side housekeeping/helper job for a lady near the campus that was disabled.

She was about 15 years older than I and had a back injury and that's why she couldn't clean her home or do much. I quickly became friends with her and she would let me stay long enough to get through my studies without interruption.

Ah-h-h, peace and quiet at last.

In exchange I would cook her dinner and do some light housework. She also paid me about $20.00 a week to do this so it was a win-win situation for both of us and kept me sane.

One Saturday morning back at the apartment with my roommates I had to go to the bathroom in the middle of the night really badly. When I opened the bathroom door I saw a naked guy and a totally strange naked girl asleep in the bathtub. Gross!

Well human nature was more demanding so I just quietly slid the shower curtain around them and proceeded to do my deed. Try to concentrate on using the toilet with that crap going on. Aha, I believe I just stated a pun!

These everyday parties were really starting to get on my nerves so after suffering through it over 9 weeks I decided to talk to the school counselor to see if any other living arrangements could be made or doubling up on studies to graduate early.

Luckily I was able to double up on my coursework and graduate three weeks earlier than the rest. Thank Goodness! **I'm Outta Here!!**

I couldn't wait to get back home! Well the next day after graduation I flew home. Now you would think the family would be happy to see me at the airport? After all I was gone over two and a half months.

Well it wasn't anything spectacular, mom and dad came to get me. I ran over to hug them and mom pulled away and made comments like, "you gained some weight over there."

I was taken aback from that comment instead of "Hi sweetheart, congratulations on graduating" or "It's great to see you." I don't want to expect too much yah know. Sheesh.

I have to think about this. My brother was now out of the house and so was I. My sister was graduating and leaving in a year leaving my folks with only 4 children at home.

I guess they were thinking of finally having more peace and quiet. It's so odd that being only gone a few months how strange I felt near my folks.

There was a huge separation feeling. The family connectivity was not there anymore. It just didn't feel like home anymore. Know what I mean? Not sure why.

So along those lines I actually felt like I was intrusive guest and had better start getting independent pretty fast. I took my luggage downstairs to my bedroom and noticed other stuff in there. My sister ran after me and said this was her room now!

I was so tired from the stress of the last couple months and traveling that I slept on the family room couch down in the basement. It was perfectly comfortable for my use and I stayed there a long time. It wasn't private during the day, but I had my own private bathroom down there.

I was hoping being away and gaining my airline certificate would have made my family proud of me. Maybe they were but I felt like a stranger staying the house I lived in for years. Isn't the old saying "blood is thicker or was that mud is thicker?" I don't know I get confused with the whole family devotion thing.

Well I still didn't have enough money to do anything about it. I couldn't leave. All my friends moved so I couldn't try to room with them. I had broken up with that boyfriend. I pretty much was on my own. Waa-Waa-Waa

Then to add to my depression of feeling welcome and lost, my mom handed me with another terrific responsibility. She felt I was an independent adult now and urged me to start paying her rent because I was using the laundry machines, showers and eating their food. Not that I disagree with her, but dang...I needed time to be employed first.

My Mom thought $20.00 per week was fair. Now that may not seem like a lot to you now, but it was a lot of money back in 1972.

If anyone knows my mom, she never lets a topic drop until it's resolved. That actually was a good thing as I had picked that up from her as well. Even now I don't let something go until it's resolved so it has made a positive impact on my professional career as well. So it's all good mom. ♥

While they were telling me all this they also handed me the airline school tuition bill that was due. They paid the down payment of $150, but I had to pay the remaining balance which was $2500. Well they did pay for my flight home yah know. They are good parents, I was just under pressure.

I truly had no clue that I was going to have this debt. Am I angry? No-I totally understand it. It was just the timing with no job yet. I feared even more surprises would find its way to me.

This was my first experience with "real grown up" pressures in life. I look back now and in a way it was all good. It forced me to make decisions and changes that are part of living independently. When you have responsibilities especially monetary you tend to move a lot faster to get it resolved.

There were times I felt pretty hopeless, full of stress and pressure. What was I going to do? Dang! The town I lived in had a huge industrial park with one very large company that probably employed over 10,000 just in our town alone.

But we also lived about seven miles outside of the city limits in the country. So transportation was also a consideration. I didn't have a car.

I knew I had to get a job fast and I was fortunate enough to have saved about $145.00 while in airline school. So I was able to purchase a Ford Falcon for $75.00. Remember those little cars? It was a sweet little thing and in pretty darn good shape for the money.

Can you imagine buying a decent car for $75.00 today? You might be able to purchase a tire for that! Those were the days my friends.

With a car now I first focused on utilizing my recent schooling and getting myself to the major airlines. Unfortunately those were in Detroit and Chicago so driving every week got mighty costly. I could only do this twice before I was almost broke.

I stood in long lines among at least 300 other candidates for hours trying to get an interview to become a stewardess. I never did get to a desk to talk with anyone. I would drive home so depressed and stressed from standing in line all day.

You see back then you had strict airline regulations and guidelines such as; you could not be married; weigh over 125 pounds; absolutely no blemishes; no children and had to be at or above five foot eight inches tall. Sounds like they weren't asking much right? Hey now wait just a minute.

My two roommates were just 5 foot tall and overweight. Why did they even bother with the classes? H-m-m-m-m. Maybe the sales person didn't release that little tidbit of a qualifier as I'm sure their parents never knew either.

I qualified in every aspect except for my teeth that were not perfectly straight. But I felt that wasn't a hindrance.

Again I never got to speak with anyone and never heard back from any of the airlines I corresponded with so I resolved the fact that working in the airline trade wasn't going to happen anytime soon. I even tried our little airport until I wore out my welcome.

I was so sad about that especially when you see the variety of short, fat, messy haired stewardesses now. No limitations like that anymore.

So after driving to the airlines a couple of times it started to become too costly driving so far and my dream was slowly shattering. Plus after nearly depleting my savings, I decided to try a different avenue since I was down to my last $29.00.

I started looking in the local newspapers. Since I had a car I could drive to surrounding towns within 30 miles.

I decided to look for something right in or near my home town. I didn't care what it would be. A grocery clerk, housekeeper, waitress….anything. I needed to work period!

After diligently hitting the pavement one day I saw an ad in the local paper for a travel agent. I applied, interviewed and soon after I was fortunate enough to gain employment with this local travel agency.

I thought, wow, I'm still in the airline business, I'll meet tons of important people and be able to travel. YES! That's the ticket….oh boy, another pun there!

Whoa Hossie!

Not so folks! I found out that this was an awful-not as glamorous experience as advertised!

Just think about it…there were no computers then so we had a six inch book of flight departures to look through and then another six inch book of flight returns.

The pages were very thin and delicate just like in the bible. Probably over 1500 pages in each book. You were not allowed to wet your fingers to move the pages because after a while, they would dissolve the data so we use the ole rubber finger!

Then you manually hand wrote out the airline ticket and ran it through a charge card type of machine. The old ones that were carbon copied. Yes, you got it…I'm that old.

I was in charge of booking flights for executives at this very large global company in town. I sat in a two person room that was dark, no windows and most days I was the only one there.

All I did was set up the reservations and book them when the booking agent handed the order to me. I didn't even get to talk to the customers at all.

I never went outside or met anyone. I even ate my lunch in the same room. TOTALLY UNEXCITING folks. It was so dark and quiet in that room. Couldn't have any lite music or conversation. Who would I talk to? I was the only one there half the time.

At that time I was earning a whopping $1.69 per hour. So my take home pay after taxes was $48.00 per week and my mom took $20.00 of it for room and board leaving me a mere $28.00 each week for gas and anything extra.

I'm not blaming my folks for starting me to be responsible. Mom's right, I was eating the food, washing my clothes, not paying for the heating costs. It was just a difficult time for me.

I was now an adult and if I didn't leave the nest egg, then I needed to compensate as if I had left. A lot of you are disagreeing with me, but I must tell you it was the best "push" my folks could give me to face the world without being in complete shock. It was still cheaper than an apartment.

Well after four months of working as a travel agent processor, I decided this wasn't for me and I ended up quitting to my parents disappointment.

To make my parents even happier, I felt that home wasn't home anymore and decided to move to a much larger city where I had some friends there. I'm being sarcastic, they didn't feel I was ready to move, but since I was now 19 I needed to find my independence.

Also being a young, energetic 19-year old at the time I felt a larger city would hold more opportunity for me. Good concept, right? Oh man….you would think so wouldn't you? But I was so frustrated that I had to do something very different and leaving my home state was it.

I wasn't worried about the city and knew the "good" nearby neighborhoods to reside in at that time. I had done a lot of babysitting, housekeeping and while working at the travel agency

I saved up every penny I could muster up. Over $600.00 which was enough to make a major move.

I had no real possessions, just some clothing and pictures so moving could easily be done by car.

I contacted my friends in this big town and they were thrilled I was coming and agreed to house me for a while. I was also very fortunate to gain employment right away as assistant manager of a dry cleaning store. Within 5 weeks I had my own apartment. Things were working out….so it seemed.

Soon after I met my first husband then and to upset my parents <u>even more</u>, after a short courtship I decided to marry him. I was NOT a mature 19 year old at that time and I never really ever had any strong parental guidance on making good choices. Again my parents had their hands full with 4 boys and 3 girls.

My folks were very busy, dad worked 12-16 hour days and mom worked all day and sometimes nights too. The older kids were in charge a lot and all too often we really needed to be directed at times. My sister and I pretty much ran the castle.

Chapter III

Well the decision was made, I was getting married. Let me tell you this was not one of my better decisions.

My soon-to be husband was 13 years older than I and very savvy. He was extremely handsome, smart and witty. He resembled George Hamilton with that noticeable tan. A salesman by trade and had been at his job 15 years at the time.

He had a very nice condo all the way up on the 28th floor, a car, cabin on a lake and motorcycle. Who could want more at 19?

We were married at a cute little church in the big city and had the reception at the condo in 1975. Well it didn't' take long but this ended up being a very, very bad idea, as I later discovered he was a mentally and physically abusive person.

After a couple years of marriage I realized what a horrible mistake I had made. But I still stayed with him. Why do we do that?

I know exactly why. For one thing we are very young and co-dependents to those we love or care about. We are also afraid. We are always put in a position of non-independence. By that I mean we never have any money to leave and I know controlling husbands ensure that.

Plus these guys are psychologically smart with brainwashing and threatening you if you leave and so on. And I was so weak and vulnerable then. I believed everything anyone told me.

I had absolutely zilch in confidence. Where would I go anyway? I didn't have any "real" friends anymore. Just casual friends, not anyone I could burden with help. Or at least I thought anyway.

But you can only take so much abuse and something gives way. You start plotting a plan to leave them. Survival kicks in.

So luckily I was paid in cash (small companies could do that then) and I began to start holding out on a portion of my pay and hiding it in the apartment for emergency use as I knew I would be needing it someday. (Just like in the movie "Sleeping with the Enemy.")

After a year I left the dry cleaners and found another job as a waitress in a prominent restaurant. This was a very famous restaurant and just working two days only, Friday and Saturday nights I made $150.00 in tips and wages.

That's great money for the 70's era and at that time we didn't have to claim any of it like you do now. I liked it so much I stayed on for two more years until my husband made me quit.

But it would last long as my husband had me quit it when I asked to work more days and also because a couple of times the chef would drive me home. The Chef was nice looking, very young but he was married with kids and I have never given it any thought so my husband put an end to that by stopping my employment. Wasn't that nice of him? Obviously my husband was not confident of our marriage or of himself.

Not only was he controlling but he was paranoid too! A great combination if you ask me!

But I was at least smart enough to tell my husband I only earned around $125.00 in tips and stashed away the extra $25.00 for two years. It's that internal survival thing we all have. I used the ole "hide it under the mattress" trick and it worked.

He never looked under there which surprised me with his paranoid personality. Or maybe he thought I wasn't smart enough to hide anything there. Who knows?

I found another job which was very exciting. I worked in a prominent hotel as front desk and switchboard operator. Now this was in the days where the switchboard was HUGE and you had two connecting wires. One for incoming calls and one for transferring the call to a room.

Just like in the show with Lily Tomlin playing a switchboard operator. "Number please."

It was a grand hotel where I met so many famous people. Some from old shows like Cheyenne, F-Troop, MASH and of course The Monkeys! I was so lucky then. You younger folks won't even know these shows that I'm talking about.

I did this job for over 2 years and had a blast!

My husband and I had been married 4 years by now and unfortunately besides the continuing physically and mentally abusive lifestyle my husband also started to drink excessively and with that used threats whenever he could.

I mean he was drinking ¾ of a fifth of whiskey every day. He also smoked 4 packs of cigarettes a day. I used to have to wash my windows weekly just to be able to see out of them with all that smoke.

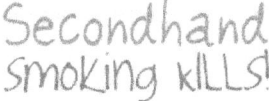
Secondhand smoking kILLs!

There were cigarettes everywhere. I can remember him taking a bite of dinner and then take a puff on his cigarette; another bite of food; another puff. E-w-w-w-w!

You know I never showed any sign of this bad relationship at work. No one had a clue this was happening. I think it was because you didn't want to be labeled or fear that friends would stop being close to me if I revealed it. I had no mental support at all and yet I persevered.

The marriage was faltering fast. As it declined, I would save even more knowing that there would be a point of no return as it was just getting worse. Wherever I could muster any money up like grocery money or change from when he had me buy him cigarettes.

I would have dreams of how I would leave, when and what would I take. Where will I live? Be careful, always be careful.

Then my husband was offered a management job meaning we would transfer to another State to run an office for his company out there. Another dumb theory I had was a move is what we need right now. Of course he'll be nicer in another State...a change is what's needed.

And shortly after in 1976 at age 23 I had gotten pregnant. What? Oh Man! How does that happen? Even better, a baby on the way...now I know he's really going to change, right?

What was I thinking? Especially with our relationship as bad as it was? What was I trying to hold onto? Why do we think outside or inside events will change people who haven't changed in years?

How many woman count on that? I hear it all the time and just shrug now. What does this have to do with someone's relationship? If it's bad to begin with, it's going to be bad no matter what happens.

But I'm a person full of never-ending hope and being young, with no real guidance possibly thought there was a chance of change. Later on in this book you'll know that being so optimistic actually has given me skills to guide companies in "Change Management." We'll talk about that later.

You know this reminds me of when my daughter or other kids always say, "You have no idea" or "You don't understand" and that we can't relate with their issues. Are you kidding me? It's the same stuff darlings - just a different year.

I have to tell you how "pregnant" stupid I was. At my first doctor visit they asked me to bring in a urine sample. Well I filled a pint jar full and covered it with aluminum foil. You should have seen the looks I got from other "seasoned" moms in the waiting room when I walked into that office. I was so embarrassed!

But I had a very caring doctor who recognized my ignorance and pulled me aside to give me a great talk on so many motherhood things. I truly am thankful to that man!

Well things only gets worse folks. During my pregnancy, my husband started having an affair with his secretary. You betcha! It didn't take anyone <u>else</u> much to figure it out as he was evidently showing it off in public at work.

But dang, I was so-o-o naïve that I just didn't catch on and here I am pregnant. I had no clue because he made every effort to hide it by being nicer so I thought the move and baby theory was really working. We were actually in bliss for a time.

Now remember I truly didn't think he was doing anything wrong. The staff at his work would always stare at me cautiously when I came in. They knew but I still didn't get it. I just couldn't believe he would do this as he was so good to me lately and we're having a baby for heaven's sake!

But I still had all those past memories that I couldn't let go of so I secretly kept saving as much as I was able and keep my security stashed in the mattress for a "just in case" scenario.

And I was feeling really good knowing I had this nest egg growing. Isn't that awful to feel that way? That's not a marriage. We should be trusting each other.

What if he was having an affair? Why was he being nice to me for such a long time? BECAUSE HE WAS HAVING HIS CAKE AND EATING IT TOO! That's why yah big dummy.

All these thoughts poured into my brain causing me to feel even more insecure. It's an awful feeling not to feel solid in your marriage.

One day he got a birthday card from her and it was a bit overly affectionate in the handwriting department. I asked him about it and he would laugh saying she's over dramatic and it's absolutely nothing.

He would tell me she's trying to brown nose the boss is all. He would then hug me and kiss me. Again, I wanted to believe him, but something seemed a bit fishy with all these signs. I just couldn't prove it and really didn't want to.

I needed to stay because of stability, my child will need a father figure, I didn't have a job, blah, blah, blah. All the wrong reasons to stay in a bad marriage. Did I miss him when he was away from home? Not really. Did I get excited when he got home? Not really.

I obviously didn't love him like I should. I feared him because he was still the one in control and I was getting so tired of being afraid. And God forbid, what kind of father figure would he be anyway? What was I thinking?!

He would bring home candies and flowers. He even bought me a 1965 Mustang. Well dang!! That settles it...he has changed, right?

That was the ticket, a new car to shut my concerns up. Well it worked. I believed him and when I went to the office his secretary would hug me and get me baby gifts. Now I really felt like an idiot. I'm so ashamed of myself thinking those bad thoughts. All that worry for nothing.

His secretary was married and had two little kids. Invited us to their house for get-togethers. I began to think all this suspicion was just rumors or just trying to gain attention of some sorts. I felt so much better about it. (Tic-toc, tic-toc).

Just before our daughter was born they hired a new office person. She was an assistant bookkeeper and we were closer in age and got along beautifully.

Then a beautiful moment, my daughter came into the world. My husband was even with me in the birthing room holding my hand and cried when they laid her on my belly. An emotion I hadn't seen in him. Was I starting to fall back in love with him? Was this the change we needed? I could only hope so.

We got her home and we showed our new baby girl off to neighbors and friends. My husband even bought me a security camera set so we could monitor her from our bedroom. Can you believe that? This really was turning out great!

Here it comes…..about six weeks later, my friend, the new bookkeeping office person called me and started telling me that she felt we were very good friends and it was her obligation to let me know that my husband was acting overly affectionate with the office manager.

UGH! My stomach, my head….Oh boy…here we go again! Things seemed so good lately. She said she was only looking out for me and stated, "You want proof, then come out here before he gets here and watch." Oh-h-h-h, get that gun out!

I felt that this was so-o-o stupid as our relationship was really nice lately but that voice in the back of my head wanted to know for sure. Besides she has never lied to me and was a really good friend.

So her office was kiddy corner to my husbands and at a certain angles you can see just about everything through her door without him knowing he was being watched.

I didn't want to do it at first. I wanted to believe this wasn't the case and I probably could have just let it be, but I kept thinking and envisioning my future. The doubting had to stop so this was the only solution.

I waited days before getting the courage to go over there. But I finally went to her office before he or any of the staff got there.

I stood in the corner and there really was no way he could have seen me without walking all the way into her office which he wouldn't anyway. My heart was pumping, I was breathing heavy hoping this wasn't true. Oh my aching head!

About one hour into the day he shows up. About 15 minutes later the office manager shows up in a very pretty outfit....and...oh damn....unfortunately my friend was right.

He didn't even shut his office door. I saw them hugging and kissing in the office. You could see him groping her butt and kissing her breasts when she came in to get his coffee.

I could hear him tell her how beautiful she was and that they were going to dinner that night. Even other salesmen would walk in his office while he had his arms around her.

They nonchalantly said hi to both of them while they were being intimate at the same time! WTF?! Like it was a regular thing. I was numbed, felt so stupid and mad at my stupidity.

They all went to lunch and I snuck out to my car which was a few blocks away. I drove home shocked, no thoughts at all in my head. Just wanted to get home (and I mean way back home).

Sure enough he left a message on our home phone earlier in the evening telling me he was working late....I sat at the kitchen table and couldn't even cry. I was so mad at myself and tired of the whole damn thing. My only salvation was my daughter, the support of my girlfriend and my hidden money.

I didn't tell him I had positive proof by being in the office. I didn't leak out that I physically saw him but I again confronted him when he got home.

You could tell he was getting more aggravated with my questioning him, but he didn't want to ruffle any feathers and being the natural born salesman he was kept telling me that all the rumors are to just get under his nerves and that anything reported to me was just a slight flirtation for her benefit.

He tried telling me that all the guys in the office do it to her. Maybe he should have reworded that to **"All of the guys do her."** He insisted he was actually working late and even brought me paperwork to prove it. He sure is a planner-not!

Don't worry folks….I didn't believe a damn word. I didn't buy it and didn't want to argue with him. I had seen it all. I just said okay and went to bed. He even had the gall to say HE was tired of me constantly questioning our relationship.

I wanted to SMACK him! HARD! Don't you twist it around and show no accountability.

By then I was 24 and already totally worn out. My little one was only three months old and still I felt I didn't have enough money saved up so I still couldn't make a truly sound decision of leaving just then.

Really though, if I had to I could have left, I just don't know why I didn't. There's that co-dependency again.

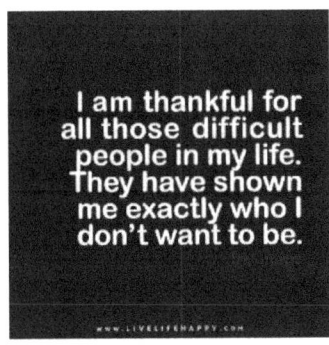

I lived with it like most women do but with the dream of moving on as this wasn't working out. I also thought of divorce being such a failure to me. I never thought I'd be divorced. I felt I was stuck with this miserable S.O.B.

But as I was getting older I really started getting wiser. I realized my constant questioning made me look insecure and I decided that I needed to change and portray myself as a confident woman. I needed to focus on my life and what its outcome might be. What you do now can determine your future.

Oh it's about to get good folks….

About another month later, sadly my husband's *"sweet and dear"* office manager/girlfriend made a **HUGE** bookkeeping error costing the company 4 months of profits and they eventually removed my husband from that facility and took his promotion from him.

That will teach you not to mess with the help. Look what it cost you stupid. The whole office shut down and people lost their jobs. My friend at that office moved onto another job and just like that we had to move back to the cities in two weeks.

Unfortunately this move made him even an angrier man. He took all his frustrations out on me. It was obvious our relationship was going off the deep end and so he started threatening that if I leave him he'll keep the baby. With this new abuse I started to gain weight, about 35 pounds to be exact. I was totally MISERABLE!

I wanted to work and he kept me from it. That's another way of keeping you dependent on them. But luckily he saw we were getting behind monetarily and agreed to let me get a job...got that?

He LET me...I know that's awful but that's where it was then at least in his mind. I was glad to be back to work as it would give me more resources to move eventually and keep me sane by not being in that house all day. You see he was able to work from home on the phone so I needed to get away.

After work one day, I came home and had stopped for groceries. I walked into our apartment and saw that my husband was noticeably drunk.

My daughter who was now 6 months old was crying profusely. I asked him why she was crying and he said he taught her about fire by lighting a match under her hand until it burnt her. That was it!! **THE LAST STRAW!!**

There's something about a mom who would sacrifice herself to an abusive person but never, <u>ever</u> sacrifice the child! The marriage was doomed forever at that point! **DONE!! I wanted him hurt badly!**

We had a two story loft apartment with the bedroom upstairs. So that very night while he was sleeping off his drunk on the couch downstairs I quietly packed a couple of pillow cases full of clothes, bundled up my little girl, and grabbed my emergency stash of cash and left through an emergency exit inside the bedroom closet upstairs.

I knew I couldn't walk down 28 stories holding a baby and clothes so as I was going down the emergency stairs I decided to stop two floors down and get on the elevator, praying he wouldn't be in it.

I was so relieved to see it was empty and rode down the remainder 26 floors to see the doorman who doubles as security guard and asked him to call the police.

This doorman was probably 70 years old, but young looking for his age. He took me very serious and immediately called the police. While sitting in the apartment office I called a co-worker who was a girlfriend to ask if I could stay with her temporarily and she agreed thank goodness, then I waited for the police.

The things that were going through my head were spinning out of control. What will I do? Where will I end up? What's going to happen to my child? Will he find us and hurt us? Help…..

Handling something like this alone is horrible. I couldn't even think of being relieved because of all these fearful thoughts. About 15 minutes went by and my husband must have awoken and noticed I and the baby were gone. He came down to the office to see if I was there.

The doorman immediately stood in the door and blocked him from getting near me. He told him to stay away, that the police were coming. My husband just looked down, turned around and walked away. I was actually surprised by that response. I was so grateful to this doorman and just like that started to shake uncontrollably and burst out in tears.

It was like all that pent up physical and mental abuse pouring out of me. I was married to this S.O.B. for over 6 years. This is when the relief started kicking in. I finally felt protected and FREE! The doorman was so nice to hold me and my little girl until the police arrived.

Now these policemen were great. Very supportive and couldn't stand abusive guys. My one and only girlfriend came and got my daughter so I could follow the police back up to my apartment to get what I needed under their protection.

We went up and I saw my husband sitting on the couch crying, then telling me the apartment would be available the next day to take anything I wanted. He begged me to reconsider and I asked him if he could guarantee not hurting me or our daughter again and said he couldn't make that guarantee. Are you kidding me? And you are 13 years more mature? Man!!

Not sure if I am sure

or not sure

So much for wanting to change your life and try to be a better person. Instead I get a "No, I don't think I can" response. I couldn't feel bad for him, I couldn't feel anything for him. He had been and was a total stranger to me. So finally HE was the hurt one.

That was it. Finished. All those years of mental threats if I left him were null and void. He never did anything. I was free at last so after six years of marriage (if you call it that) I became a first time divorcee (at my expense) with a one year old child.

Chapter IV

I was mixed with emotions, sad for this to happen the way it did, but happy it did as that was a horribly long six years of more misery than I care to remember.

While staying at my girlfriends, I started looking for another better paying job right away and noticed an ad for a fulltime cashier supervisor at one of the prominent groceries in the city and thought that would be an interesting and fun job with a possible solid future.

I applied and low and behold I got the job. I was also able to set myself up in a small apartment one block from the store and in the same building established a really nice babysitter. Maybe it was all finally coming together.

I worked there for two years and really enjoyed it. But it I found out later it wasn't to be a long-term a career choice. I had some awesome memories there though. I met a bunch of super people. A couple of my meetings resulted in dates which was nice.

One was a famous radio announcer for one of the largest radio stations in the city and another was an owner of a famous established business and now owner of many retail stores.

These were guys just wanting to date and I certainly wanted to hang onto my independence so it was mutually great. No pressure dates but boy did I ever get treated royally at some of the restaurants.

I remember one time as I was cashiering and an 80-year old millionaire would frequent our store and when he would lean over to pay for his purchases he would drool into his shopping bag. It always grossed out the baggers. All of us girls in the store would laugh about it.

I ended up having to kick him out of the store for shoplifting mints at the counter several times. I think he did it just to gain attention since he was wealthy and obviously very lonely.

A few nights a week I would make extra money stocking the shelves and those nights the owner would let me bring my daughter with me who was now one year old.

She was so cute helping me work. She had a blast in her nighty and slippers running up and down the grocery aisles. He would let her pick one thing each night to keep. I kept hinting "take the steaks" but for some reason she went for the candy. Go figure! Ha.

I have to tell you and a lot of you single mothers will relate to this. It's awful damn hard to raise a child or children on your own. There is so much daily pressure that at times it's unbearable.

If she got sick I had to leave work and some bosses don't like that. If she had a bad babysitter, I had to find another and wonder if that babysitter is good with her. I would often think while I was working what they were doing, is she having fun, is she safe, are they hurting her?

I had a couple of very bad babysitters and when I found out and think about it I wish I had done more to protect her.

It's nearly impossible to work a fulltime job and not feel guilty about it. My kid didn't have a dad and 9 hours a day she didn't have a mom either. <u>To this day I will never forgive myself and always feel guilty of that</u>.

When she had a school event I'd miss it because I had to work. If she wanted to do something I couldn't because I was so tired from working all day and on and on and on. I wish I had stayed on welfare because at least I would have been with her every day, raising her, teaching her and protecting her.

It breaks my heart every time I remember it but she's 38 years old now. Our relationship is close and good. I am thankful to be able to talk to her and see her often.

Back to my cashiering job.

During that time I lived in an apartment right across from the store. Very convenient but at night not one of the safest areas to be in. This particular area used to be a prominent and very safe area, but in the later 70's it changed quickly to being more crime ridden, dirty and corrupt.

One day I picked up my almost 2 year old daughter from the babysitters and walked that short block to my apartment. My hands were full with my holding my daughter's hand and carrying a full bag of groceries in the other with my purse on my shoulder (shoulder bag type).

This nice young man was inside the apartment building in the front lobby area standing near of one of the apartment doors as if he was waiting for someone to come out.

I didn't think anything of it. There were a lot of people in that apartment building. He was very professionally dressed and kindly opened the door for us which I thought was nice of him since I had so much to carry.

My daughter and I walked toward the elevator as I lived on the second floor and as we got in, suddenly his foot shoved inside to jam the door from closing. He then put a 3" x 9" knife to my daughter's neck and asked me for my purse. Yah, he was nice alright! NOT! I was so freaked out that I peed my pants.

My poor daughter whose eyes were bugged out cried out to me. I immediately handed him my purse and luckily he left us. I couldn't imagine if he had followed us up to our apartment. What would he had done then?

When you read all the things that have happened to me you will for sure think that an angel has been with me the whole time. I have to believe that or how would I have survived?

We were stunned for such a long time. I can't even remember how I got off that elevator and ran to our apartment. I was so fast trying to unlock the door and get us inside.

I grabbed my daughter and hugged her so tight. What a horrible thing to happen. This neighborhood was no longer safe for us.

Evidently the thief's intent was only to get some quick cash. And gosh darn it, I just got a $250.00 cash bonus from my boss for Christmas. All my credit cards and banking information was in that purse!

Geez, can't I have a year of no stress, safety, peace and quiet? And to think I just unloaded that gun and put it back in its holster.

But most importantly about that whole deal is that my little girl was safe. I hated that she went through that at such a little age. She tells me now she doesn't remember it at all which is good.

What?!

Now I lived only a half block from the police station and when I called them, it took the police over 40 minutes to get to my apartment. I could have walked it in 3 minutes!

Dang! They were slower than turtles. Should have hoped for "Ninja Turtles."

When they <u>finally</u> got there, (a male and female officer), the whole time I was giving my statement, the male officer was yawning. That was certainly reassuring.

The female office wasn't very caring either. She kept telling me to shut my daughter up from crying. I felt like I was interrupting their break or something. Anybody got a donut?

Since I didn't feel protected in that neighborhood anymore, the following week I decided to move back towards a safer area of town. The landlord was not cooperative because I was breaking my lease, but I was fortunate enough to get it sublet so he let me go.

We found a huge one bedroom apartment and I lucked into a really great babysitter right in this new building and this safe neighborhood. I really do have good luck (sometimes). This neighborhood was known to be very secure compared to other areas of the city.

About six months after our move the grocery store was totally destroyed by a fire. There was suspicion that the owner's set the fire and paid off the cops so they could collect the insurance, but it was never proven.

Uncanny that all seven cash registers were opened and each held $500 in them. There was no money residue or anything to indicate burnt cash. I figure someone went in before the damage was done and cleaned it out.

Also the safe was wide open and I used to do the nightly books. I know there was always around $10,000 in that safe but it was completely empty. No one had any evidence of being pried open. As if someone had a key and just opened them.

Whomever it was, they at least were smart enough to grab up all the steaks first too. Every piece of meat was taken out of the coolers. Now that would have been your first clue that this was pre-planned? Huh? My kind of person! H-m-m-m. Something's fishy in in the Big City again. Nope! They left all the fish.

Well I was ONCE AGAIN left without a job, a single parent, with bills to pay and getting more exhausted with this whole scene anyway. I am so tired folks….

The crime was moving more towards my good area and getting increasingly dangerous. I didn't want to raise my child there anymore so I decided to move back to my home State to be closer to my childhood friends and siblings.

Whether it was the right thing to do or not I at least knew it would be safer and more affordable. In the late 70's, early 80's this Big City and suburbs became even scarier.

Chapter V

I didn't want to ask my parents for help so I had a best friend from high school that I stayed in touch with offer to move me back home. Best friends are awesome!

I really didn't want to do this because I knew that the jobs were scarce back home, but security and being near my whole family of friends, siblings and cousins were more important to me by now.

I was moved relatively easily and found a low income apartment within walking distance of a major portion of businesses and downtown which was great since I didn't have a car anymore. Yes, the ole Ford Falcon and Mustang passed away long ago.

Actually that's not true, Falcon died, but the Mustang was kidnapped. I was gone one weekend and when I got back my car was gone. VANISHED! I had the keys, but my ex-husband had the title. I told him and he didn't seem to care so I just let it go.

After I settled into my new apartment, the very next day I went to a couple of hiring agencies downtown and the unemployment office. Right away I was able to at least gain a six-month state contracted position with the Department of Natural Resources.

The only problem was I needed another car now because the location of this facility was about ten miles out of town. I thought about this carefully and knew no other jobs were out there so I took the remainder of my savings and went used car shopping. My landlord knew of a neighbor boy who was selling his car so I walked over to check it out.

I found a Chevy Vega. Remember those? This car was in terrible shape, but for $350.00 you couldn't expect a lot. It rattled and rolled, but that rust bucket got me around reasonably. I started having panic attacks because I ran completely out of money by then.

Luckily my landlord knew of my struggles and came over with a whole box of wonderful food and cleaning products and a little cash until I could get on my feet again.

She even brought over a little girls slip and tiny ballet shoes she found in a rummage sale. It fit my daughter perfectly. All day she pretended to be a ballerina.

I started to cry. Wow, there are some really sweet and caring people out there in the world. She knew I was good for it. I paid her back by raking her lawn, trimming bushes and some light housekeeping for her. My angel is always helping me.

Now working for the DNR was an awesome position. I was the office administrator do I did a little bookkeeping, human resources and reception work. I would give out fishing and hunting licenses.

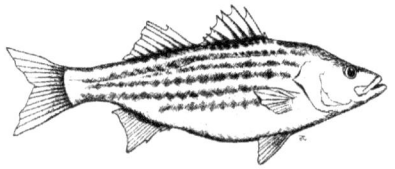

Sometimes our DNR chief would walk in the office with people handcuffed for cutting green trees or setting illegal traps. Oh so exciting! These guys would hang their heads down low and they would wait in our office for the police. I was always nice and offered them coffee or a handcuff key…..ha.

It was difficult looking at them while they were being processed. These were normal great people who just didn't follow all the forest or hunting rules.

Sometimes a person would bring in a dead fawn or a dead snake found in their home. It was our job to analyze what happened to them. That was a gross part of the job as they came in plastic bags and smelled to high heaven.

One time there was a forest fire and our DNR agents had to drive through the woods seeking it out. As they were driving a pilot in a small Cessna plane would radio me with the coordinates of the fire and the ground crew so we could direct everyone to the fire.

Needless to say this was a very exciting office position, but unfortunately it had to end as the six-month contract was done and the State funding for it was done.

I did such a great job they tried extending it, but couldn't. I was so sad about it. What an adventure that was.

ONCE AGAIN I was back to seeking work but couldn't afford the waiting so I had no other choice but to go on welfare for a short bit.

Welfare? OMG...I don't care what anyone says, being on welfare is so horrible. Paying for your food with food stamps while others watched is humiliating.

Others would look at you wondering why I can't get a job. I know because I did the same thing. Experiencing it yourself truly brings you back to being humble and not so judgmental about it. Luckily I only had to do this for 2 months. Don't get me wrong, I think this is a great service for those in need and I was personally in need and thankful.

But those looks you got from others in stores, even cashiers was piercing. What I should say is "Shame on them" as one day they might be in the same predicament. I was very thankful for this service, but felt so dependent on others. And the system then was so darn difficult.

This is when a welfare agent would literally come to your home and look through all your cupboards, closets and mark down everything. They were checking to see if you bought any new furniture or jewelry or other substantial stuff as that would reduce your welfare income.

They were also looking for men's clothing to see if a guy was living with you or giving you support. It was so awful then! I had to drive to the welfare office to check in weekly and collect my food stamps and this office was 10 miles away.

I saw so many underprivileged and depressed people. Tons of them. I wanted to think of a way to get them back out in the workforce and feel productive again.

For something inexpensive to do I would take long neighborhood walks with my daughter who was now 3 ½ years old. While walking I came up to another man walking and we began to talk. Soon after we found a lot in common and started to date.

He owned a very nice ranch style home near my apartment. He was an engineer for a subcontractor working at the town's nuclear power plant. He didn't have any children. He was very handsome and tall but was a bit "out there" and aggressive in nature.

By that I mean he likes to take risks and does the extreme like skydiving, snowmobiling up a steep cliff, climbing mountains or checking out haunted homes. But he was incredibly sweet to my little girl.

He treated my daughter like she was his own. Even bought her a swing set and carved her name on it. She loved him so much and I really think he was smitten with her in a fatherly way. He would be so good with disciplines and showing her why it's wrong.

He was teaching her life's basics and it was all good. And my daughter adored this guy! Even to this day she talks about him fondly.

Sometimes he acted like he felt he owned the world and no one could tell him any different. I think that's a man thing. But again he was super to my little girl so we dated a couple of times a week and it seemed to work out. He had his place and I had mine. No pressures and pure independence. It felt great!

I was being still being very cautious as the horrible memories of the past were still fresh with me and I kept thinking to myself it was just dating, nothing serious, right?

Since I still hadn't acquired a job yet, I was getting unemployment, and during all this time I didn't sit idle. I kept applying every day...everywhere I could. I eventually found an office manager position at local small business. I applied for it, interviewed and got the job (Really?).

At the same time, my Chevy Vega broke down and the repairs exceeded the value of the car so I turned it in for parts and got back $50.00.

I needed a car as this business was also a few miles out of town. The man I was dating offered me his old van he had on his property. Sweet deal. Ugly and rusted but very dependable.

Things were looking up. You would think so but unfortunately it does get worse (heavy sigh). I had been at this local company about eight months doing all their customer service, ordering supplies, bookkeeping and personnel. Trucks coming and going. Staff in and out.

Boy I hate starting this…..here we go again….it almost hurts to keep telling you, (huge sigh).

Wouldn't you know it that one of the owners started flirting with me? At first I didn't think anything of it. I've seen him flirt with all lady customers so it was no big deal. I was only 27 at the time and being the only girl at this company I was used to the guys joking around about ladies and making flirty remarks.

I had crooked teeth so my confidence level still wasn't 100%, but thankfully accepted any and all flirtations as long as that's all they were.

But ultimately the flirting became more and more prevalent by the fact that he always kept the guys out of the office and damn, then he started stroking my hair, asking me to lunch, stopped by my house with ice cream for my daughter, giving me money, buying me gifts, and so on. At least I had enough sense to recognize this was becoming more than simple flirting.

He was also married to a super sweet lady and had three kids of his own so this was very uncomfortable for me. But that damn positive outlook I have kept me thinking this too shall pass. Who am I kidding?

After a couple of months of this right around the time I figured I had better say something, he had asked me to lunch and began a very serious discussion with me to the point where he was thinking of leaving his wife.

That was serious now! Damn, I needed a job bad but not this badly. Whoa! I immediately stated several rebuttals on why this wasn't a good idea and how bad I felt which he didn't agree with.

He thought he was the most perfect man and just couldn't understand why I wasn't more attracted and receptive to him. **BECAUSE IT'S JUST WRONG DUDE!** Yah you're cute, but not that cute!

When you are young single mom depending on her job, it's just a horrible position to be put in. I decided the only way to solve it was to quit because it was getting more uncomfortable to work there.

After working there one year and knowing the right thing to do, while I continued to work I did the pro-active thing and started looking for another job. Gosh….AGAIN?!

When I told my boss I was quitting he was devastated. He tried and tried to tell me he would not flirt anymore, but I could tell that there was a little obsession thing going on.

After I quit he would stop by my townhome a lot. I had to stop this. Many of those days I would purposely invite girlfriends or neighbors over so I wasn't alone. So after numerous lengthy discussions he finally did stop showing up.

I thought I had actually saved his marriage by talking to him and leaving BUT I later noticed he hired another young pretty lady with similar features me and I started to chuckle. It's their problem now. We are targets for these types of men ladies.

Someday this guy's going to lose that entire business and you know who is going to be the new owner? You guessed it...his wife! She'll get it all! (And righteously so).

Doggone it, I really liked the job so this was unfair to me but I had no choice in the matter at the time.

Now the man I was currently dating had no clue about the flirtations of my boss. I didn't dare tell him as I feared he would react wrong.   I knew what I had to do and it would quickly fade away anyway.

At that time the local nuclear power plant was also blossoming with employment opportunities. With the recommendation of my now serious boyfriend to his boss who was subcontracted with a construction company there, I was able to acquire an office position with this same contractor. Such sweet luck!

So Onward-Forward…..

My new job title was Office Administrator/Human Resources Assistant.

<u>Yup Folks! My very first official professional human resources office job!</u> Waa Hoo! This is really where my career in human resources finally began. I was the office and human resources administration for this engineering firm who consulted for the construction company at a nuclear power plant.

By this time it was 1982 and my whole life changed with this new role. Not only did my pay go up 30% but I finally discovered my career passion in HR. It was a terrific work environment too. There were none of the vast laws we have today so it was an employer's world and we were loving it.

I worked out of a construction trailer with eight engineers. Had to wear hard hats, steel toe shoes and get x-rayed coming in and out of the facility. No kidding, it was really great!

Now this was just one construction trailer of probably 1,000- or more of them with over 4,000 people working there building this new nuclear power plant. So many construction trailers you couldn't see past them all. They were lined up for 2 miles.

It was a female's paradise as for every one woman there were 5 men in the population. **"It's raining men ladies."** Muscular, wearing hard hats, tight jeans, all of them looking just like the man of your dreams! Yum.

Who is this guy?!

This particular contracted company that I worked for was home based out of another State. They were very generous with pay, schedules, benefits and training.

I jumped from making $4.75 an hour to $7.50 an hour in the late 70's. That's a sizeable increase in those days. This company even sent me to the big city I moved from for a week to learn several types of software training. (Déjà vu).

This was the first time I was educated with Excel spreadsheets, Word documents and database systems. Now if you recall, this is when computers were very large and some had keyboards still actually attached as one whole unit. Remember those bad boys?

Backup tapes were the heavy 12" reel to reel type or floppies. No laptops existed yet, at least none that I knew of. Calculators still cost $50 - $100 dollars which is a far cry from today's cost of $1.00.

I loved learning all these new programs and just kept wanting more and more. This training opened up so much opportunity for me. Each session was easy and I adapted relatively quickly making the engineers and my boss very happy. It was the type of job you just couldn't wait to wake up and get ready for. I even made a ton of new girlfriends there.

After being together almost two years I eventually broke up with my boyfriend who also worked there and that was a good thing- trust me. If I wrote about my time with him, I'd have to write another book.

But I will tell you just one funny incident. (Really not funny at the time, but the ending certainly made ME feel really good).

He was another wonderful man that also cheated on me…now why do they do that? I was a young, beautiful, thin, tall and basically a long blonde haired chickie in those days. Plus a lot of fun to be around.

What is it with these guys? Well I can say when I met him to my knowledge he was faithful. A little after a year together is when it got shaky below.

I guess he also wanted to be experienced in diversification like I eventually was. But not for the same reasons. That's one thing I can say is I've never ever cheated on a boyfriend or husband.

Not even that bad one I was previously married to the first time. I was faithful to the end and it feels good knowing that. Cheating will get you nothing but heartache and most times can be deadly (if you read the papers) so don't do it! Okay, getting back off my soap box.

Back to this ex-boyfriend…..

Well one week he and the other engineers were supposedly on a business trip in Europe. I thought it would be nice to surprise him when he got back so I got to his house very early the morning before he was to return and went to his house to pre-decorate it. I knew he was due back around noon so I got there around 4:00 am as I had a lot to do.

Oh Poop!  There's that crap again.

What the hel-l-l-l-l!

Well it looks like he got back already. I was so disappointed not being able to surprise him. I check on the house every day and no cars have been there for 2 weeks. All of a sudden two cars are in the driveway. Now I started to think of all sorts of things on his behalf (there's my damn optimism coming out).

Maybe it was a co-worker that just decided to stay there for the night. Or another engineer dropping his car back off or a family member visiting…..something like that. Yeah, that's got to be it.

Possibly he may have caught an earlier flight with another engineer that drove from the airport together and just crashed at his house. Yah that must be it too. Keep convincing yourself.

But once again, the hairs on the back of my neck started to crawl indicating that I just <u>HAD</u> to make sure. Trying to maintain positive thoughts here folks.

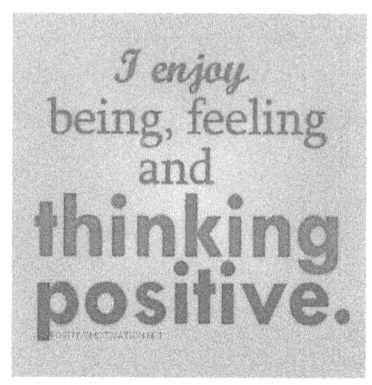

I had a key to the house so-o-o-o I quietly snuck inside. I didn't hear anything and I didn't see anyone in the kitchen or living room. No bags, nothing.

I thought, okay, my earlier synopsis was right. Someone followed him home or helped to drop his car off and maybe the other car was one another engineers. It' going to be okay. (Letting out a big sigh of relief).

Oh-h-h but as I slowly and quietly walked toward his bedroom and peeked inside….. **HERE IT COMES….GET READY…….BAM!** YOU GOT IT! Back hairs are flying now people!

(Heavy, heavy sigh…) Here it comes…ready?……**I saw him in bed asleep with another young gal.** <u>And there were no jammies on folks.</u>

I took a step back. My mind was racing with frustration, anger, betrayal, all that junk described in romance novels. Not again!

Wait just a minute……now wait just a minute….hold on one second….this gal looked awfully familiar to me. I looked again and took a moment to think.

Yup that's right she used to eat her lunch with some of us at the communal picnic tables onsite at the nuclear construction site. She worked for a different company at the same location. I also knew that this particular gal was quite young and wore braces on her teeth. Pretty darn plain looking too if you ask me. What is wrong with you men?! Dang!

I took a deep breath and slowly started to sneak away from the bedroom door. God…not this again….. Here we go…I'm numb, can't hear, can't see, swirling mind……want to scream!

I WAS PISSED!!

After regaining my composure, I was quietly passing through the kitchen when I also noticed my boyfriend's wallet on the table. Whoa, a moment of opportunity comes to my mind.

Being a seasoned and experienced rejected woman by now I thought to myself like any woman would that this S.O.B. owes me! Yah! Get mean, Get back, and Get even!! Okay, I've calmed down.

I had been with him a long time (over two years) and dedicated my heart to him and so did my daughter who is not going to understand this at all when I explain why we broke up. A little girl is not going to comprehend it. (I wouldn't tell her anyway until she's older and only if the subject came up). Little girls need little girl thoughts and that's just the way it is.

So as I stared at the kitchen table I opened his wallet and luckily he had a ton of cash in it. I took out $260.00 in twenties. Don't worry, I was nice about it and left an I.O.U. note inside with his new girlfriend's name on it. See I can be fair while being depressed.

I knew it was over with us so I decided to do the only right thing I could do. I took that money and went to the 24-hour drugstore to buy every last stinking dental floss they had. I also purchased about 16 vials of toothpaste. Can't have floss without toothpaste now can we.

Then I went to another store and bought every one of theirs. You can actually get a stockpile going with that kind of money back then. I easily filled a large grocery bag full.

I got back to his house still very early that morning (I knew they were still asleep as no lights were on in the bedroom). They probably partied pretty hard the night before so they wouldn't be up for a while. Poor things. Yeah right!

It was still dark outside and I had to be very quiet about this whole thing. I proceeded to unravel all of the dental floss in HER car. Must have been over 40 rolls. I twisted it all over her radio knobs, put it in her windshield washer tank, around her tires and just everywhere I could see.

Took me a good 30 minutes while keeping an eye on the house. There is no way she could get inside that car without cutting the floss off.

I then took the toothpaste and used that for HIS car and squirted away. It actually made a neat pattern on the car interior. Threw some of that in his windshield washer too. That took another 20 minutes. I was getting exhausted with all this fun!

I left a note to both stating they shouldn't forget to floss or brush when they're done! It's important to maintain good hygiene isn't it.

That was it! Finished. I actually felt great about it as it didn't cost me anything and it took all the frustration away. I also ended up with a little cash left over so it was all good.

I walked back towards my townhome with almost a gait strut whistling. Then when I got home the reality sunk in. Thinking I'm a failure in relationships once again. But I KNEW for a fact this time it wasn't me.

It's the type of guy I always attracted who just wants it all and I mean IT ALL! I'm very nice and always go for these strong, confident types. Learning to be a bitch does have some advantages and I was educating myself fast.

I took the remainder of the money and bought myself a nice new briefcase and took my daughter out for breakfast that morning as I felt things were going to change for the better.

I would hear back from my boyfriend's family that evening telling me how sorry he was and how much he missed me.

Even his ex-wife of 9 years begged and pleaded to take him back. Are you kidding me?! So what people! Enough! Who really cares? You made your bed, now lie in it…(another pun folks!). I'm on a role with puns!

I explained the situation to my daughter who just loved the heck out of him as best I could as she was only 5 years old. So unfortunately it was best to lie and tell her he was moving to Europe and we couldn't go. She was sad, but eventually understood.

I hate lying to her, but what do you tell a 5 year old? Later when she was about thirteen she brought him up in a past conversation so I felt it was time to let her know the truth and it all worked out.

I felt so powerful after that. Going to work I held my head high as I didn't have anything to be ashamed of. My heart heals very fast when it comes to a cheating spouse. Any and all intimate feelings go out the door after that.

Alas, it does get worse (are you kidding me?)

The next day he pounded on my door of my townhome demanding I return his TV. I told him to go upstairs and get it. He literally ripped it out of the wall. I also gave him a nice portrait of me and he gave that back with all kinds of nasty words written on it. I ended up calling the police just so I had a report on the whole in my wall from the TV.

Men act so childish when they get rejected.

A few days later I would still take my walks with my daughter and sometimes he would be in his yard. Unfortunately his house was in the direct walking path so it was unavoidable.

Once in a while my daughter would wave at him and he would wave back. But he never tried to contact me after that. I had a great job, a nice townhome, a beautiful daughter and nice friends. I became more and more "tough" with whatever life threw at me. I was on top of my game.

I couldn't wait to see that girl he cheated on me with at work again. I'd occasionally see her walking around...I'd purposely sit at her lunch table and start to talk to her. She wouldn't say anything. I wasn't unfriendly at all. I WAS OVERLY FRIENDLY on purpose. It was my way of showing her how independent I felt. But looking back at that today, it was childish of me to keep "egging" this on.

It was obvious I was still mad, but I finally stopped and moved on. She eventually stopped showing up and I later found out she quit her job. I certainly didn't want to do that to her but I can't blame myself for that.

She's a big girl making her own decisions in life. I found out later that she was the one who lured him into bed but again he was an adult in a relationship and knew better.   It's called "commitment."

She also knew he was seeing me so I don't feel bad for either person.   I think later she felt bad about it, but was too uncomfortable to even talk to me. Maybe she has learned from this? I don't think so. That was a pretty bold thing to do.

My now <u>ex-boyfriend</u> would come into the same construction trailer, look at me but would not say a word. The other engineers knew about it and actually stood by my side. Boy, it felt so good! I purposely dressed in the finest tops, jeans and had my hair so perfect. I even lost another 15 pounds so I was looking and feeling very sharp ladies!

Now again this job I had was one of those jobs you loved going to everyday and becoming independent again was making it even more enjoyable. I had no desire to start up any new relationships.

Time for me and my daughter to bond! I started to make more girlfriends and concentrated on doing many more things with my daughter and maybe start crafting. (Boring right?)

I had a couple more dates, but by now I just wanted to do what I wanted and not have that extra baggage to deal with. I just couldn't trust a guy right then. Needless to say working and having siblings, girlfriends and co-workers was my life saver that kept me going.

I started putting in more hours on special projects for the owner and at times I think even the owner of the company was smitten with me as once a month he had fresh flowers delivered for me.

What a nice guy. I'm telling yah I was really peaking in "cute" at that time. But no more boss relationships so I kept my distance and it worked out terrific!

My boss was single and tall. I mean 6 feet 5" tall-yikes! He was very successful since he owned the business and had two young sons. He always wore corduroy pants. Ewe, remember those? A lot of elite college Professors wore those. He had somewhat of a "nerdy" look. His hair was so out of control! You are so not my type at all.

Now I'm not overly beautiful, but I was very pretty then and my personality which enhanced my looks was what guys liked. My particular personality got me in a lot of great places and careers in my lifetime. But it also gifted me with all the bad ones.

This nuclear construction site was all hard hats, jeans and over 125 outhouses everywhere. Yup, even portable toilets as no plumbing was installed yet. Nothing but the best! I bet they had to pump those outdoor toilets daily with that many people using them. Think about it…4,000 people every day!

With this new career, I was getting trained on new software and learning new things like preparing payrolls, maintaining personnel files, confidential blueprints and handling the day-to-day inquiries.

I began to realize my passion for this type of work and thus I concentrated on this for my continuing professional career.

One of my biggest memories and shockers was where I had to type a 160 page document starting on a Wednesday to be done by the following Tuesday. It was a technical engineering proposal for a particular construction phase for our company.

If this document did not get completed by the end of Tuesday, my boss would lose a $255,000 contract. That's typing approximately 23 pages a day folks. Holy cow! Well we were going to give it a good try!

So the engineering team worked diligently and they kept handing me the written procedures and I kept typing. The next two nights I had about 48 pages done. As I was typing away the janitor was cleaning the construction trailer and all of a sudden my computer went <u>BLANK</u>! **OMG…Dead Silence!**

My face also went blank, my mouth dropped, my chest froze, I screamed and I stood up to see that the janitor had accidently unplugged my computer while he was cleaning. His face was in horrible shock as well.

Now since I was brand new with computers you would think I should have periodically saved my work instead of waiting at the end of the day? You would wouldn't you?

Nope, I didn't. At least not that day's work. Tears ran down my cheeks. I lost about 24 pages for the day. All was not lost but I was devastated by the set back. I had to leave and take a short walk outside to regain my composure.

Thank goodness my best friend was my babysitter. These were times of long hours and weekend work. I hardly saw my daughter and that was so painful for me. Knowing she was in safe hands made it a bit better though.

I persevered and came back onsite and picked it up where I left the night before. Each night I stayed until 2:00 AM to get ahead of the task. By Sunday morning I had 99 pages done.

Now each time I finish a section, I had to print it and give it to the engineers to proof and many times they came back with corrections or changes.

This was why it took even longer to get this project done. We only had a few more days to finish 70 or so pages. The pressure was mounting.

I went home at 5:00 pm on Monday to be with my daughter for a short while and get some sleep. I woke up at 9:00 PM and went in to keep going. My boss was there proofing the work as I went along and would periodically hand me pages needing rewording or had technical language errors.

I diligently typed away, getting up every half hour to shake my hands and get the muscles stretched but also to <u>SAVE MY WORK</u>.

Ultimately by 7:00 AM on Tuesday morning **I GOT IT DONE!** Spellchecked it, put in a nice presentation binder and gave it to my boss who then drove me home since I was visibly shaking. He was forever grateful and I hit that bed like it had been months without sleep.

I didn't have to go in until early afternoon the next day and my babysitter dropped me off since my car was still there from the night before.

I got back and no one was in the construction trailer so I did a little of my normal job, but I still felt numb from the previous heavy load.

That day I was confident my boss did his presentation beautifully, but I didn't hear back if he had gotten the contract or not. No one heard anything for several weeks which worried me and everyone was tense about it. I think he did that because he wasn't sure about the contract either.

Then a few weeks later I received a cute container of nuts that said **"nuts about you"** on the outside.

When I opened the container there were six $100.00 bills mixed with nuts in it with a note thanking me for all my efforts from my boss as he **got the contract**! I was so proud of myself. All the other engineers received bonuses for their input as well. Those were grand days indeed.

Back in 1982 that was a lot of money for me and being a single parent, it sure came in handy. I loved this job and my boss and most of the engineers were good with me. Since I needed another car I bought my sister's for $500. It was a Gremlin! Yah Hoo….those were so popular then!

About a year later the biggest construction company in the world announced that this whole nuclear power facility was shutting down and all 4,000 plus employees were told to leave by the end of the week.

Day by day you could see many exiting with their possessions in boxes. Each and every one had to be escorted out of the security area individually. That was so time consuming. Most had to wait in line for long periods of time. Some brought chairs to sit in as it was that long of a wait.

It was a massive thing to see. So many sad faces. That parking lot became empty by Friday at 6:00 pm. That's how fast things can happen sometimes. Blink…..it's gone.

This might help you understand why this happened. You see they put this nuclear construction site on swamp land and when they built the heavy containment buildings, they noticed they were starting to sink and tilt, much like the Leaning Tower of Pisa.

A bunch of us would take pictures of each other next to the containments and tilt our bodies to match the buildings.

Sounds funny, but it really wasn't. The construction company had to think fast, so they installed some type of equipment underneath the containments that would freeze the ground holding them up.

When I would walk out of our construction trailer, you could see these huge silos with steam spewing out of them in mass amounts from putting the water into the ground underneath and freezing it. It was quite a sight and noisy.

Now I was told this was a cost of over $20,000 a day to keep the ground frozen. This was probably a major reason the construction of this site went way over budget by a tune of $25 million plus.

While the site was closing down my current boss had other business contracts elsewhere in the Country and offered me to continue on with them. I was honored to be asked, but this meant moving to a large Eastern State that I've never been to and as a single parent with no family nearby, that just wasn't in the cards for me at that time.

He really wanted me to reconsider it and offered to pay me more than I'd ever imagine and some of my moving expenses. Even his sister called to try to convince me, but my comfort level was strong back home and I was not willing to take a chance like that. It just wasn't good moving me or my daughter that far away just then.

I wouldn't be near any family or friends and that was important to me at that time. I will later find out that this was not a good decision and I should have accepted.

The nuclear site was never reopened again. I went back 10 years later to see it and all the buildings are corroded with thistle and weeds growing everywhere. Much like a ghost town. Even the containment buildings were still tilted but no more than before.

A 40 million project turned into 4 billion dollars later and never did become a working site...sad you know. But it opened my doors to even greater adventures.

The following week after the facility shutdown, a job fair was hosted on the construction site by several other nuclear plants within nearby States.

It was a huge job fair. Must have been over 100 companies in representation. I circulated the tables and handed out my resume. I was fortunate enough to land an interview for position as a Word Processor for a company in a nearby State. Actually a direct hire to the electric company in that State.

I received a call to interview and got the job. Yes, I know, it meant leaving my friends and family, but it was a lot closer than the Eastern side of the country.

I would still be able to drive back and see my family and friends over a weekend as I was only 5 hours away. I could manage that and besides I was out of a job so I had to do something fairly quickly.

Chapter VI

You've got to be a super woman to be as flexible as I was. I always had some type of emergency funds at this point. But think about how stressful moving like this was. Whole new State, new company, no established friends or babysitter. It was a staggering two weeks to get all this going. But I managed it somehow.

We packed up our items and went off to a new adventure. Just after moving there and getting my child enrolled in elementary school, just 8 weeks later I had also gotten into a horrible automobile accident with my daughter who was 5 years old at the time.

I was on my way to her school as she was in a school singing event. We started singing in the car and I wasn't watching the road in front of me as I kept looking at her while we sang. I smacked into the back of another car at 40 mph's.

I almost lost my little girl. I can still remember seeing her head stuck in the windshield before I passed out. She wasn't wearing a seat belt as we were driving 8 blocks away which was so bad on my part. Never get complacent with driving. I was so stupid then!

In fact my inside dash radio flew out of the back window. That's how strong the impact was. I remember screaming and then passed out. **I will never forgive myself for that**.

I just started my job so there was no time off accrued and management was not very understanding at all so they wouldn't allow me to leave early to get to her at the hospital which was an hour away.

Oh by the way my current car was a Chevy Chevette. They were not big cars so it was totaled. I had just paid it off and now I had to start over with yet another car as the accident totaled mine. I just moved into my apartment and didn't know anyone except my babysitter who ended up being very helpful getting me around.

I had no cash to put down on a car so I had no choice but to lease one. This was just another terrible time for me!

You know what the most horrible thing I can remember about this? And I tear up every time I say this. When I was on an examination table in the emergency room the nurse told me my daughter was okay.

I looked at her perplexed and said "who?" The nurse gave me a terrible look. I actually didn't realize I had a child right then. I was like staring blankly at everything-I couldn't comprehend anything anyone was saying for at least an hour.

Then I started to lose it. I cried and shook uncontrollably like you've never seen. Finally the doctor told her I was in shock. I went over to my daughter who seemed okay, but they were taking her to the big hospital in the city because she had some internal bleeding going on. I was able to go with her in the ambulance. I just kept bawling over that.

My daughter was in this major hospital an hour away from my job and I had to work at this new job all day in pain and bruises trying to concentrate on my work and thinking of my little girl constantly.

I felt terrible not being able to see her until the evening hours, drive home alone and not have her in the house. This was excruciating for me.

What was even worse was when I did get to the hospital to see my little girl which was around 6:00 pm, the nursing staff would look at me with such evil in their eyes because they just couldn't accept a parent not seeing their kid until the evening.

They would daily tell me how these other parents were there all day with their children. I felt hopeless about it. The guilt in my heart was overwhelming. That was so mean of those nurses.

They would recap her day and say stuff like, "You would have enjoyed it if you were here." They didn't know what I was feeling or how badly I wanted to be there. I had so much emotional pain that it was hard to do anything and stay sane.

In a way I was glad I was working to keep my mind occupied. But being a newly hired employee there was no room for sympathy and understanding. I was even limited to so many phone calls to the doctors. So heart breaking!

This word processing position was also at another construction site in that State. It started out well, but sitting at a desk retyping

technical documents over and over was not my ongoing career choice for the future.

You ever use a word processing machine from the late seventies? Where you have to type in the space symbol and have certain codes to the text? Again, very old and antiquated equipment. Keyboards were attached to the screens still like the old days.

After working there two months, I could recognize which staff were part of the "in crowd" with the supervisor. There was a definite click in the group. These gals would shoot rubber bands at each other, play loud music, and goof around most of the day. Try concentrating on your work under those conditions.

You see here's how this job worked. The idea was that we would receive merits for typing the most words each day. These merits could be used to get out of work early or add to a day off without using vacation time.

Kind of a weird way of measuring production but I was really happy about it as I needed all the time I could muster. With that said, I became very competitive with assignments. Almost to a feverish tone.

I soon witnessed a little game being played between the supervisor and her "favorite" merit receiving staff. She would hand a select few the larger documents and the others would receive the 2-3 page scrapings.

It was a very lucrative plan until several of the team members started to complain. The more they complained, the smaller the size of the documents were received. I kept quiet and tried to figure out a way around it.

I decided to get to work earlier than the supervisor to grab as many of the larger jobs as possible and hid some under my smaller work so I could accumulate more merits.

When the others came in, they didn't have any work right away because all the larger jobs were siphoned to the "chosen" but I had my little stash tucked away every day.

Well here's how stupid I was. You see we have to sign off on all the documents we typed. The supervisor has to report this back to the powers that be in order to calculate merits.

The supervisor started to realize what I was doing and put an end to that by announcing she would be the only person to hand out jobs going forward. So much for trying to be an opportunist and beat the favoritism system. I gave it a good shot!

Well many more unethical things were happening such as the "chosen few" taking much longer breaks, sitting around talking more, coming in consistently late or leaving an hour early with no action taken. One of the gals was late an hour every day for 6 weeks.

To add insult to this they would flaunt it in our face by literally stating "too bad you can't get away with what we do." Come on people!! What the heck is this? This was disheartening as two other really good workers came in late three times and they received a verbal warnings.

The politics were so thick and spread out to others that it was worthless to bring any of this up so I kept my nose out of it and just did my job every day.

Here's the neat part...it got to be so-o-o-o out there with these atrocities that I started to giggle a lot. It was just too damn funny and utterly ridiculous!

I had to form some kind of outlet as it was hard seeing the favored ones continually get whatever they wanted and much more.

My giggling became contagious and some of the other "righteous" workers started to giggle whenever these gals would pull off crap. Maybe my confidence was spreading to the others as the good workers started to sit near each other and form a bond.

Okay, now the supervisor took notice and was becoming curious by this. She walked up to one of the gals asking why she was laughing and this gal stated because of the comedy show she's able to watch all day. (Meaning their actions).

Oh Boy...not a good thing to say. That gal's on the trouble list for sure.

The supervisor got back at her by moving her to another department. For a while after we all calmed down and just did our normal jobs. It was going along fairly nicely but the back of my neck started to cringe as it seemed too good.

It was! I was at a desk next to the supervisor's one day and you couldn't help but hear their conversations because they were so LOUD! A lot of times I think that's intentional.

I found out how they were able to double the merits and rip off whomever was paying for it! Which I assumed was the customer. The supervisor would count large documents as being totally redone when all they did was fix one or two grammatical errors. That's it!

They were like big rats in the corner feverishly figuring out all kinds of devious plans. It's a faulty program that upper management truly didn't think through and it was costing the company mega bucks. Like I said this was very educational for me and I soaked it all in.

I could tell I was learning a lot more about these things and growing much wiser, more mature and my "don't give a damn" was coming out. Unfortunately with this new education I was learning deception and but I knew the difference. I actually felt sorry for them as they only had each other, and that was pitiful!

And the language was unbelievable in this department. A bunch of immature, gabbing, rude, mouthy, unprofessional, ridiculous women…ah-h-h-h-h saying that felt good.

About one year into my job, I came into work and saw all of them cowering over the supervisor's desk whispering. I didn't think anything of it as that's their "norm" every morning. I noticed they seemed to be looking at some smaller pieces of paper with some scribbled handwriting on them.

I just assumed they were trying to figure out how to get more merits out of the system and were contributing their ideas on paper?

They kept looking behind them and had a sinister gleam in their eyes as if they found a treasure chest. Then the supervisor approached a few of my peers and asked each one individually to sit by her desk and write a phrase on several pieces of paper.

Now, picture this, her desk was wide open, no walls around her. Just a desk in front of all of ours so we all were visible to what was happening.

As I was minding my business, not paying attention to my surroundings because I was basically tired of all this stuff, she finally got around to me. She towered over my desk with squinty eyes.

She looked like Esmeralda, the witch and abruptly asked me to go to her desk. She then instructed me to write a phrase on several pieces of paper. I have to chuckle because three of her other buddies were standing behind her watching all this.

I think one was drooling, yuck!

Where's the big white lamp, smoking interviewers, whips, and a reverse mirror like you see in cop shows? That's how it looked and felt folks. I couldn't figure out yet what this was about so I played along reluctantly because I knew no good was going to come out of it.

Torture isn't all bad - depends who is doing it.

Well after I wrote on paper three times. I glanced over to the other sheets they were clutching like diamonds and they slowly spread them out. Dang! It was clearly evident that they were **not** my handwriting. I write much larger than others with a beautiful cursive and this was scratchy, tiny writing.

The supervisor then asked me to read the precious notes and watched me do this. As I read the notes, my reaction was shocked! Did you know that someone else was taking notes on all this unethical conduct…….wow I wasn't alone in this. But who was it? I wanted to read the others, but the supervisor grabbed them out of my hands.

Unfortunately for me they found the notes in a drawer of a desk I normally sit in more than half the time so **I** was chosen as the victim since they couldn't prove who did it and since I never associated with them, I was **targeted** (outsiders always get picked yah know).

You see each desk had a different type of word processing machine on it so we would rotate at times depending on the job.

I probably sat at this particular desk 3 out of 5 days. Another gal sat at it the other days and she was also very quiet.

I <u>insistently</u> denied being the culprit, reshowed them my handwriting comparison and explained that I have stayed out of all their crap. I didn't want anything to do with it. No involvement period!

Once again, I was pissed and this time demanded to see an upper manager above the supervisor as I was seeing where this was going along with the accusation. Okay, don't do that people. It just gets you in more trouble.

This click group were like nervous pigs in a position ready to attack. They literally leered at me and stood side by side each other. I hate being in this position, such immaturity. This is how riots start. People cling to each other the same purpose even if it's wrong. They don't stop until it's too late. Known as social frenzy.

The supervisor blurted out "no, you did this and changed the handwriting on these notes just now". **Are you kidding me?** I randomly faked my handwriting just now? What the hell?

I began putting the atmosphere together and I figured they were actually scared that someone knew their antics and this might just get to the President of the company or someone who will take action. THEY WERE WORRIED!

People in fear do forceful things to make them <u>not</u> look scared. They act braver, try to draw at your weaknesses, get their comrades to back them up. A lot like bullying.

Aw hell, I'm sick of this so I went to my desk. But I even pulled out my old notes with my handwriting when learning how to run the machines back a year ago and my handwriting in different cursives, did not look like the ones they showed me. I laid those on her desk. Damn, should have made a copy as she grabbed them and tore them up! There goes my evidence.

How could she deduce I was this person? She told me I was going to see the head honcho in HR. I'm so-o-o-o scared-NOT!

So a bit later she marched me down to this "Big Guy" or the **Human Resources Manager!!** I'm typing that in bold so you can read it as if you were a big radio announcer. Now say it like a radio announcer with an echo.

The Human Resources Manager!

Now this guy was about 67 years old, about 200 pounds overweight (yup he was the big guy alright) and you could tell he was a gluten for punishment (besides food). The type that get a real kick out of making others feel inferior. He had a very large head with tiny eyeglasses. Looked like that guy in Mad Max. It fits!

As I was walked in, he began to set the tone immediately by leering at me when I was escorted inside. I have to tell you that **he was damn ugly**!

You could feel the "mean" in him. I immediately felt warm and fuzzy all over. Believe it or not, I had never met this guy ever during that whole year. That's what I call a "Great HR Manager – NOT!"

I sat in the chair across from him and I looked up and noticed that his office walls did not go all the way up to the ceiling so every conversation could be heard. That certainly made me feel this would be private.

He stood up, leaned forward placing both his hands on his desk. Now get ready for it.....**BAM!** He screamed to the top of his lungs approximately 2" from my face stating, **"Who the hell do you think you are?"**

He yelled so loud and feverishly that he spit all over my face. Great! Another facial to enjoy. I knew at that moment all eyes were on his office door as you could hear a pin drop. I was back in the ridiculous mode and pretty much had enough so I played along. Let the show begin!

I responded as I should have "I'm a Word Processing employee here John and I'm baffled why I'm here." "If it's about the notes, I didn't write them as you can plainly see and I demand to know why you feel I did." You don't DEMAND with this guy. That only set him off even more. The veins in his face were ready to pop out!

He told me to **SHUT UP** and told me to never call him by his first name. I then asked him what I should call him, Mr. HR Manager. He then claimed that I was spying on the whole group and that I wasn't going to get away with it.

Okay, now what a ridiculous thing to say. I'm so baffled by the fact he is wasting his time on the frivolous claim. Isn't that what he pays his supervisor for?

He got so red and flushed that I actually started to laugh…which truly didn't make it any better but dang…he was ridiculous looking, huffing, puffing and wheezing.

I again told him that it wasn't me who wrote the notes and he said he didn't care that they were found in my desk and wanted my security badge.

Now wait a minute. Whatever happened to verbal, written and suspension warnings? I've never been counseled with this company, been an exemplary employee. Oh, I forgot….we're still in the days where you could do all that.

I told him I would get a lawyer and he said "Get your damn lawyer." I knew this wasn't a win-win situation so I handed my security badge over and came to the conclusion that I was no longer employed at Fantasy Island.

I really didn't care as it was and had been a complete joke there for so long. Five others before me moved onto other jobs for the same reasons, but I must be a gluten for punishment.

Maybe I just like stupid and ridiculous people. Who knew? I still think I was in a co-dependency mode and just couldn't get to that place of being totally secure and independent yet.

Then just like out of the Wizard of Oz, a very nice and gentle older lady came to get me so she could escort me off premise. She had a soft demure and voice just like the good witch in Wizard of Oz.

I don't know why but I tried to explain myself and she told me it would be okay and confidentially that she knew who wrote the notes, but that nothing could be done about it and that pretty much was that on things.

I pleaded with her because it was my job and most importantly my integrity and she said "it isn't going to happen and you never heard any of this from me." She went on to explain that I was young and will get over this and find a better job. Yup, this isn't Fantasy Island it's Ellis Island.

She was so soft and eloquent. I wanted to slap that b@#ch. This was still an era of where bosses could do lots of unethical things. Chances of winning a case were slim then. Not like it is now.

I never touched the papers in the drawers that were there all along so if I had the brains to clean it out once in a while this would never have happened. Yet another learning lesson.

Protect yourself at all costs. But who would have known? Really now.

I just don't know. I've had such extreme stuff happen on jobs that maybe this is how it's supposed to normally be. I'm sure I was an escape route as the supervisor as she and her gang never liked me and probably had a plan all along. You know how the nice witch on Oz would wave good bye to Dorothy with all the little munchkins wishing her bye-bye, bye-bye…….

Crap….

But I was lucky enough to know some great engineers there and they pooled together to help me figure out what to do. I was surprised at a lot of the stories they told me that went on there. Unbelievable. And these nuclear plants are supposed to be safe? Not with these people working there.

Well I immediately went to the unemployment office. I was so surprised to find out they marked me as a lay off and therefore able to collect unemployment which was a blessing for a while.

Maybe they felt guilty on how it was handled. No I don't think so or maybe because I was a single parent. Either way, I figure they just wanted anyone not in their "click" out. I can't really remember as it was over 30 years ago.

In those days it's kind of a worthless effort to pursue any action so I chose not too as I had a 5 year old daughter and felt the odds were against me anyway.

In any event, this whole fiasco will fade away into a stupid and ridiculous memory. I swore I wouldn't go through that again.

Right? Sure, you betcha.

As you read on unfortunately the pain will continue and dang if some of it isn't even better (worse).

I viewed this as a good opportunity to pursue other avenues and to just forget this whole thing. I wasn't strong though as slowly these things happening to me in life were making me weaker and weaker in the confidence and ability zone.

I had to find my career with a stable and structured company and build myself up. I had tons of integrity and stamina. I knew what type of person I was so it was really hard for me to fathom all this happening.

As I read while I type it's unimaginable for one person to go through all this, but somebody's got to be IT! Might as well be me. No really, this actually happened. I did start to think this is the "norm."

I was still a smart gal and had saved up a nice nest egg for emergencies, was getting unemployment and I was able to rebuild some confidence of my eventual re-employment.

Do you know a good way to do that, just talk to others who are not employed? Some have it much worse than you do and it gives you a sense of stamina to overpower the situation.

I absorbed all of this and took some much needed time off for me and my little girl for about a month. Don't get me wrong, I was job hunting but not to the point of stressing myself out.

I had a little time. No more stress for a while.

Oh by the way, always and I mean always keep your resume updated for anything that might happen unexpectedly. I know I've mentioned this before, but it's important.

I'm the type of person who writes down things so I can look at it later to see if it makes sense. You know, my options and such. I highly recommend writing everything out as it offers clarity on the path to take.

Chapter VII

I used to live in this one big city and thought now that I was older and my daughter older that a nearby large suburb would be the best place for job prospects (here we go again). There were a tons of highly populated suburbs with big industrial parks. All sounded good.

I did my research on these places, was able to acquire an inexpensive duplex apartment near schools in one of the suburbs. Then packed my things in a U-Haul and made the long trek back.

This suburb is about an hour from the big city. Far enough to be safe and economical. And it's a college town so plenty of jobs in the area or nearby towns.

I'm a go-getter and I don't let grass grow under my feet, so within two weeks I also landed a wonderful job with a reputable and very large lawn care company as Office Administrator/Human Resources about 30 minutes from my duplex.

It was a brand new site and a great opportunity for me. I was feeling very confident about it so I went into the role fully prepared, psyched up and strong.

This new division office had about 23 lawn care specialists, a general manager, sales manager, sales staff and a small office staff. Heh, heh, heh. Sorry that's uncontrollable chuckling as about six months into the job I'll be doggoned if the crap didn't start again with this new position.

See working in human resources or office management can be fun and exciting! You ought to give it a try! I'm trying to sound like those old military recruitment ads. Come and explore a career full of great adventures!

Are you warming up to all this? This is another doozy. Please take me out of my misery. Here we go…..

You see we are the ones that deal with all the messy clean ups that the higher ups don't want to deal with and probably shouldn't anyway. But that's what keeps us hopping I guess.

Well shortly after taking this job we moved into our newly built building and got settled in. We started hiring more staff and I particularly brought onboard a gal who had such a nice soft voice for our customer service department.

Not long after her coming onboard other staff began to complain of this office person's underarm odor. **Are you kidding me? Dang!**

I'm not stupid and knew who the person was. She had the greasiest hair and her clothes never looked ironed. So what is the best way to handle this?

I would gently and casually talk to her about it and she said she didn't believe in foreign products on her skin. What she heck did she bath in or wash her clothes in then?

Still I responded as if this was fascinating that she didn't use any soap or shampoo. Not trying to pry I asked her what did she use for hygiene and she said just water. Okay then!

I've been exposed to this very strong hygienic odor every time I walked past this person so I knew it was inevitable that it would need handling. I mean it was really bad.

I was hoping more that she was aware of it too and try to mask it with something, but then again she doesn't like any foreign products so perfume was also out of the picture.

Also for some reason they never seem to notice it on themselves. Needless to say I didn't want to deal with this...who does? Why couldn't I have anything easier to work on? It's never that way you know.

After a third complaint I knew I had to approach this situation right now or my reputation of taking care of things would be compromised. Oh Geez I guess I'd better get that gun out again.

I sat in my office contemplating the right tactic to use when I approach this person. I mustered up my professional self and I cordially asked the gal if she had time to visit me in my office.

Once we were alone I started out with some useless chat regarding how things were going. It was relatively pleasant but she knew something was up. So………I *"softly"* and *gently"* brought up the underarm odor complaint to her.

Believe me there is <u>NO</u> soft or gentle way to approach this! You more or less just come out with it and do your best to maintain a pleasant demeanor throughout. I was very apologetic about it and told her I truly wanted to work this out amicably.

Well needless to say THAT DIDN'T WORK AT ALL! Hold onto your hats...here it comes again..........are you ready? **BAM!!**

She literally and I mean literally jumped on my desk, got on all fours, knocked all my paperwork to the floor and screamed to the top of her lungs that I was insane and that she didn't have a underarm odor problem that no one in the office likes her and this is just a lame excuse to get back at her.

Then she did the unthinkable, **yes you guessed it**....she shoved her armpit right up to my face and said SMELL!

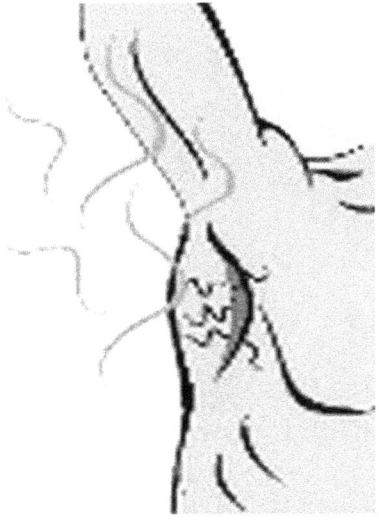

Not only did I have the audacious pleasure of smelling that delectable scent of aged armpit, but once again I received another spit shower during her verbalizing **(LUCKY ME)**.

While I was soon to pass out from all the fumes she then got off my desk, stood up, straightened her shirt and stormed back to work. My office door was wide open after she left and all eyes in the office were pinned in my direction while I was wiping my face and putting on an oxygen mask.

One secretary's jaw was opened so wide you could have thrown a football in it. When I got up and started to walk out of my office they immediately got busy and tried not to stare at me. I notice one gal had such a grin on her face and was about to burst into laughter.

I embarrassingly turned and went back to my office. I had to just sit there for a bit to collect my thoughts if there were any left after that.

I started thinking that this must be a major portion of the human resources job description. Really? Well think about it. The majority of our role is handling employee issues or personal agendas. I've handled hygiene issues for years.

I was becoming seasoned in "insanity" and it was turning into my norm adjusting to any weird situation after all I've been through so far. Are you kidding me?!! No really, I just figure this is how it is every day in business life.

Now I'm the office administrator and human resources manager so I've got to maintain a professional demeanor for heaven's sake! Get a grip woman!

And I did just that. After I wiped my face and sucked some oxygen (just kidding), I picked my papers up off of the floor and nonchalantly walked out into the main office area.

I chatted with some of the other girls and acted as if nothing happened. I then handed this same gal that spit on me and barked like a dog a FEDX package to process.

She grabs it from my hands harshly but I maintained composure and still smiled and thanked her. I then walked outside the building towards the back of the building and let out a huge scream. AGH-H-H-H-H!! Whew that felt much better.

Well a few days passed but the problem was still there. You know how I could tell? Because everyone started spraying perfume or room deodorizer every time they walked by her. She would just sneer back at them.

I felt so unaccomplished over this ordeal. I had to do something as again other staff are depending on me. Now I'm usually a person with terrific brain storming ideas, but this was not one of my better thought processes.

Here we go folks…..I had the bright idea of purchasing a can of spray deodorant and put it in her desk drawer with a kind suggestion note wrapped around it with a pretty ribbon and a box of chocolates. That should work right?

Holy Cow! Did this go over well! Here comes the insanity again!! She took that spray can and proceeded to spray everyone's computers, desks, chairs, the walls, people's lunches-EVERYTHING until it was completely empty.

All the office staff were crouching down, coughing up the fumes and just didn't know what to do. Luckily it was lunch hour and only a few were in the office when this happened. Of course she made sure I was around to see this childish act.

I was fuming and had enough! I immediately requested she go into my office for a much more serious discussion as her behavior was totally unacceptable.

I didn't care if I hadn't consulted with the General Manager or the Corporate HR. I had enough witnesses and yes, documentation of consultations to warrant anything else I chose to do.

Fortunately for me when she walked back in my office she immediately decided to quit that day. Talk about leaving on a good scent. At least we all felt protected for the day – get it? I'm so good with puns today.

Unfortunately she filed unemployment stating we made her work life miserable. Hey, just a minute….who made whose life miserable? Fortunately we won her unemployment claim based on the fact that **She Was Nuts** and we were respectful with trying to handle the situation several times and she was not receptive (yah think?).

No really it's because she chose to quit but she twisted it around saying we were at fault. I've had terrible times with unemployment law judges. This case was cut and dried but took 3 hearings to get to that point. Do you realize what that cost everyone? Such a waste of everyone's money.

Another great thing is we had enough consultation notes and witness statements. Needless to say this stinky situation resolved itself. Yet another pun-dang I'm good!

It took all of us about a day to clean up the sprayed mess and a few days to get back to normalcy if that. One of the gals in the office just couldn't fathom this happening, however as much as I had been through already I reassured her that she will soon find out that this is the "norm" in most office environments.

By the way, this is the same office where I was putting boxes in the storage closet and I looked down at some coiled wire in the corner. I went to pick it up and low and behold it was actually a snake! I screamed, I'm sure it screamed if it could.

I got a trash can and scooped it up and threw it outside. Now this was a tiny baby so mama had to be around nearby. Every day we would walk around the office making sure no strange items on the floor or in our drawers. Never did find another.

Oh and yes…things get worse….unfortunately. My gun is loading!

At this very same facility we had a remarkable and charming young sales manager who seemed to be able to sell over 50 new contracts a month making our site the most successful in the district.

I was always amazed at his determination and drive. He would come into the office every day in a crisp suit and polished shoes. He was witty, confident; very sales knowledgeable and had a lot of drive. He managed several salesmen who idolized his success. This guy was going places (oh you betcha he is).

Now this sales manager gets commission ahead of time on sold contracts once their committed and entered into the system.

The general manager was very happy about this as these new sales were also a bonus for him and a reflection on the success of this new division office. All seemed good.

All the office staff were busy entering these contracts, sending letters of confirmation to the customers and ultimately started setting up the jobs with the lawn care technicians.

Since I was doing most of the bookkeeping I started to notice something wrong. I discovered that none of these contracts had paid anything in over six weeks. That was odd.

Lawn care had already begun on these contracts approximately three weeks earlier. Normally I wouldn't get too excited, but over 50 new contracts hadn't paid a dime yet? H-m-m-m-m-m.

I also noticed that a 10% discount was applied. The only way a customer gets this discount is by receiving the first two months payment in advance and then monthly thereafter until the full season ends. That was a huge "Red Flag" for me.

Well the lawn technicians were out there taking care of these new customer lawns. I finally received a phone call just as I was discovering these infractions. It was from one of the new customers who claimed they never ordered this service and didn't intend to pay after it was done by the technician.

And they kept strolling in, one-by-one. More of these new customers started to call in saying they never signed up for lawn care service either so I started to get even more suspicious. One said if this is a ploy to get us to buy lawn service, it isn't going to work. I noted all these comments as they came in.

I had to reassure them that I would do a full investigation and get back to them by the end of the week. So I decided to do some detective work and my first resource was to pull out the ole phone book and look up these customers to see if I could find anything on them like geographical similarities, etc.

Okay, this is how stupid this guy was, you could tell that all of the people were picked in consecutive order in the phone book. I figured out he would pick a page, pull a couple of names from it and then flip a couple of pages in the phone book and pick more names, addresses and phone numbers out of that.

It was so-o-o stupid and weird. Oh-Oh, I feel something bad coming up. Can you feel it? My stomach is starting to cramp, my head is aching. I'm getting that awful feeling again. But I had to concentrate on the subject at hand and got back to my detective work.

I made copies of all the pages and matched the information to the sales orders. He isn't much of a genius if I could figure it out that quickly. Wait a minute I just insulted myself. Oh well!

After a long investigation and a continuation of phone calls to and from people that stated they never ordered our service, I ultimately concluded that my detective work was a sure thing.

Well I deduced that **he turned in bogus sales**. No, really? Do they do that? Hell yes they do!

Since there was enough evidence to prove this, I decided not to bring this up to him directly for fear he would find some way of getting out of it, but instead I drove to the corporate offices with my documentation and informed the Sales Director who was his boss along with the Operations Manager and Controller.

We ended up contacting the remainder of the new customers and they confirmed that none had ordered any lawn care service which we documented. This was a loss of over $3700.00 a month or approximately $45,000 a season not to mention the bonuses and commissions paid out in addition to that.

Everyone at corporate came the same conclusion as the evidence was profound. So we talked about how to best handle this situation.

It was decided that the corporate sales director, operations manager and controller would come out to our site unannounced when they knew the sales manager would not be in that day.

They came out and took all the original handwritten "supposedly real" customer contracts that the site sales manager originated.

They also asked me to delete them from the computer system since they were bogus anyway. Then we had to write letters of apology and state some lie about a computer glitch causing this to happen and to enjoy the free lawn treatments on us.

This seemed to work as the complaints discontinued. That following Wednesday, the Corporate Sales Manager and Controller showed up to our site again when they knew the site sales manager would be in.

When they got there unexpectedly they went up to that young sales manager and told him they were excited about the new sales numbers recently and asked him to produce these new physical contracts to them so they could look them over.

Now remember, they TOOK the original handwritten contracts back with them a couple of days earlier. The site sales manager seemed very confident and said he would get them right away and went into his office.

HOLY COW-HOLD ONTO YOUR HATS! You're in for a fun ride! You should have seen the look on that sales manager's face when he came back into the main office area. He turned white as a ghost, his lips quivered and his eyes were bulging with panic. I hate to say this but **IT WAS AWESOME!**

We all watched this poor guy literally running back and forth room to room trying to figure out where these contracts went and how to produce them to the Controller and Corporate Sales Manager. I felt like making popcorn to watch all this……just kidding.

You could hear him frantically whispering to his sales mates saying things like "what am I going to do?" "Help me." The tension in the office was so thick you could cut it with a knife.

He then thought, well I'll tell them I left them at my home office and went up to one of the girls and asked them to provide him with a computer printout of these sales.

Ha-ha-ha-ha. I'm sorry, but remembering this makes me chuckle. The office person stated she didn't have them in the system anymore. He yelled, "WHAT?" "What do you mean you don't have them anymore?" She literally showed him that none were in the system.

The girls in the office couldn't really fathom what was going on as we didn't tell anyone the details and you could see they were freaking out a little over all this panic. The corporate personnel were enjoying every minute of it. They would periodically come into my office and snicker.

Eventually after a full hour watching him scramble we pulled him in my office and confronted him with our investigation. We produced all our evidence and he eventually admitted to it. We ultimately had to terminate his employment.

But we had to squeeze a little entertainment out of him first. And yes….it was worth it. After all, he screwed the company out of money and damaged their integrity. We also apologized to the office girls and explained what had happened and why we couldn't say anything.

Their mouths dropped with disbelief. One office gal said this was the best job she ever had. So much free entertainment all the time.

Again I told them we'll probably experience a lot more strange things as we age. It was at least inevitable in my career and becoming the norm for me. I don't know if they ever got their commission money back from him. Probably best to just consider that his severance.

Oh...but wait again! It's not over yet folks. After all that excitement, it finally calmed down to some normalcy. These past events were just that...the past and over with.

They eventually hired a new Sales Manager who seemed to be a conscientious and focused guy who was a bit older and had a great sales background. He also got along with everyone. He particularly developed a process where all sales would remain legit. It all works out.

Aw come on...now you know me better than that. Oh heck, I'll keep it going……here we go……….P-tang!

One day I came to work on a Saturday to get caught up on some paperwork and noticed a couple of cars in the parking lot. I thought nothing of this and felt it might be the janitorial service or a lawn tech getting his truck ready for the following week.

When I enter the building I have to walk past the General Manager's office to get to my office. I noticed that the General Manager's door was ajar and had lights on.

Again, I thought nothing of this and assumed he might be in there catching up with some paperwork too. As I reached for my office door handle to unlock it I could hear moaning in the General Manager's office which our walls literally connect.

Fearing he may have fallen, I quietly moved towards his office and arched over, then placed my ear to the door to hear what the heck that noise was. I head moaning, some soft like a female's and some deep like a man's. Are you catching on?

All of a sudden, the moaning got louder and louder. Now I'm a mature woman, so it didn't take me long to figure out that some hanky-panky was going on. Oh boy...not the General Manager. He was so nice and professional and newly married! Maybe he was showing his wife his office? Heh-heh-heh.

Shortly after, it became silent, then some mumbling conversations. What...no lighting up a cigarette afterwards? I knew they would be coming out soon so I quickly went back into my office. I didn't shut my door all the way so I could see who it was. **OMG!** Are you folks ready? Really?

Here it comes....it wasn't the General Manager at all but the **NEWLY HIRED** Sales Manager and one of the temporary office gals we had here part time. I started to make some noise by opening and closing file cabinet drawers as they started to come out.

He came in my office a bit concerned, is eyes were bulging in fear and nervousness. He asked me how long I was there. To ease his mind I told him I literally just got in the door and didn't realize anyone else was here.

He straightened himself up and gave a huge sigh of relief. He said they were there working on a special project. Oh you betcha boss man! I've got your special project right here dude!

Now I have to capitalize on this scenario with a couple of lawn care sidelines. Does this mean that they were testing fertilization concepts? Do you think the grass is greener with upper management? Maybe he was sprinkling her with rose dust…..just saying.

The following Monday, the new Sales Manager came to me requesting we permanently hire this temporary office person that he was so fond of. She had to be on the bottom to get to the top I guess.

I protested stating that we were going to be slowing down due to it being the end of the season and we really didn't have a spot for her. I didn't want to cut down other office personnel hours either.

He was the boss of that department and he convinced the general manager to hire her so with my dismay and verbal protest we did.

Well she started out okay, gave her some minute tasks in the beginning. A couple weeks later she started to come in later and later, then had a few last minute absences. Much of her mundane work wasn't getting completed. I was so aggravated that within a few weeks I determined this wasn't working out.

Luckily I had a consultation with her in my office a week ago to talk about her coming in late a lot and slow productivity. I'm a smart cookie by documenting the meeting and having her sign it. We also had a strict attendance policy in place for this very situation.

I went to the new Sales Manager, shut his door and just flat out stated that she is going to be terminated per our attendance policy which was strict if you are within your 90-day orientation period. Crap she couldn't even handle it within 3 weeks of employment!

He argued with me, but I stood firm as we had terminated others for the same infractions. I also had the blessing of the General Manager. I explained that I had talked to her I told him that her attendance and lack of working when she was here just made it worse and to remain consistent we had to terminate her.

He must have said something to her as the next morning as I found a letter of resignation from this gal under my door that morning. She evidently did not want a termination on her record and I'm sure he was an active consultant on that decision. I was happy with it as now we wouldn't have to deal with unemployment.

After she left I went into his office and shut the door. I then privately advised him to keep his personal life at home as everyone in that office knew about their affair.

The only reason everyone knew is because they were both in the office every Saturday doing their business while lawn technicians would be in and out. Also he was not private at all about advertising her as his prize trophy when he went out drinking with his buddies.

Small town news is faster than special delivery as you well know. He was an older guy and she was 23 years younger. I'm sure they had a lot in common, right? Yah right! The terrible part of all this is he also had a daughter who was nearly the same age as this gal.

Chapter VIII

Well a couple of years later a much larger firm bought this company and closed this particular site down completely. They ultimately consolidated the territory to another larger suburb.

Most of the current staff all moved to the new location including me. I had just purchased a home that I loved and the drive was about the same distance so that was a good thing.

They eliminated the lawn care portion of the business for this territory and acquisitioned the residential painting aspects of the business. Things would be changing rapidly. A whole new ball game in business. But still service oriented.

Most of us were able to keep working for the newly acquisitioned company. With this position, I was promoted into the role of Administrative and Human Resources Manager for the residential painting franchise division which was a subsidiary of the same company.

I was excited to get out of lawn care and into something totally different in a much nicer suburb. And what a professional building. Now this has got to change…….I'm pausing on purpose. Oh come on. It'll be great! I'm positive to a fault.

I managed the human resources and marketing support functions for about 125 franchise operations within 5 States. I worked out of a very nice office in a 4-story building with a very stately looking business park that had a gorgeous atrium inside. This business park was high class and everyone wore suits. It was so refreshing for me.

This office building must have had over 100 companies occupying space in it. These office suites were huge. Ours alone had 10 offices, a large reception area and conference room. My huge office (and I mean about 900 square feet) also had a beautiful view of a pond right out one of my many windows with a solar fountain and sweet ducklings.

This building was right next to a large mall and shopping districts which was also very convenient. What more could you want?

With so many franchises to support you can understand the volume of hiring paperwork for each one and I was the only person doing all of it.

Needless to say I had to get another office person to help. I hired a young man for reception and light administrative. He was fantastic for this role!

I'll give you a perspective of the work load. Each franchise had anywhere from 4-10 employees under them. That was anywhere from 600 - 750 staff to set up on payrolls-EACH YEAR! Our peak season of course was March through October.

Then we had to put together franchise startup kits each October for the next March season. These kits were the size of 17" x 24" boxes and weighed 25 lbs. apiece.

These kits contained everything the franchise leader needed to contract jobs including advertising material, calculator, cash, credit card machine, office supplies, etc.

Space in the office was limited so we stacked them to the ceiling (don't tell the fire department as that's a no-no).   Even throughout the hallways, reception area and conference room. You could hardly walk around in March.

That's over 1,000 new hire packets and 125 franchise start kits to make, process and setup. In addition, I was responsible for bookkeeping, payroll of approximately 650 seasonal employees, vendor relations and customer calls. Needless to say there never was a dull moment but my days went by very fast. I WAS BUSY!

The company that owned us and the division Vice President were from another Country. He wasn't in the office much. He expected everyone to do their job without issue and he would pop in to look over records. Why not? That's what I would expect. He was a fun guy when he would show up. So everyone liked him.

Pretty much standard in Corporate and divisional worlds. I handled everything and we had one sales manager, also from the other Country that was there daily working with his sales teams. He was also a great person to work with. I loved their accents.

It was a hustling and bustling office, full of movement, chatter and people. Very professional atmosphere, suits and ties, etc. There was never a dull moment. Always something to finish.

I was in charge of a staff of three, one was the male receptionist and two were our bookkeeping assistants. These two gals were great and terrific with the books so I was thankful for that.

Now here is where it starts to get juicy again. Okay, you thought it was going to get boring going forward? Come on now.

I've already had such a history of work excitement that I was actually surprised of this next story with all the professionalism here. I thought I finally found my path. Something can't go wrong all the time, right?

Oh you betcha it can! Here we go…..one of my weekly responsibilities was to confirm the sales report, then email it to Corporate. I would enter the jobs completed and add future projected.

Luckily from past experience as you know I saved a copy each week on a floppy disk that I kept in my desk. Yup we are moving up in the world of modernization as we now have floppy disks and separated keyboards. Woo-hoo!

About four months into the spring season I received a call from the Corporate Controller stating we had serious accounting infractions where things just didn't add up; specifically our sales numbers were off by tens of thousands.

Now I knew my records were accurate as I kept every little piece of documentation in separate account files that coincided with my spreadsheets. So I and the bookkeeping assistants audited our records for the past several months and we were indeed on target with all the documentation.

So we couldn't figure out why the Controller's records were different. I even asked to see his documents to compare. His looked right also.

As I said earlier, I kept all my software documentation on floppy disks in my desk drawer which is locked. I decided to copy these to another floppy disk and send my copies over since the beginning of the year.

I also painstakingly copied all the hard paper documents showing that they matched my records. All of this information went to the Corporate Controller. About two weeks later I heard back.

Low and behold the spreadsheets they had were not the same as the ones I sent them. I told them as far as I knew I was the only one in these files doing the data entry and could not understand why each were different from my copy.

Well through upcoming technology which wasn't much in the 80's and a savvy IT manager's capabilities we discovered a doozy.

Someone went into the system every week and usually late at night accessing the files typing in different sales numbers. We could see the time and what files they were in but that was all we could see. We couldn't identify the culprit yet.

It was logged in under my name and password. This person was pretty keen. They would first save everything on my original spreadsheet in the computer. Then do some changes and saved this new data somewhere on other floppies that were then sent to corporate.

OMG, I just thought of something, what if they thought it was me? Wait a minute, what good would that do me? I wouldn't get anything out of it. Paranoia kicking in.

The only people allowed to my password was the Site Vice President, the IT Manager and the Controller. I never caught it as I said, my records were right at least on my end.

Here's the beauty of the thing…now I always copied the spreadsheet on Fridays and put the floppy in an express envelope for Monday's to be sent out to Corporate.

I wouldn't seal the package until Monday afternoon just in case anyone else had something to go out there. I've been doing it like that for a long time with no problems.

Whomever was doing this would make their changes to the spreadsheet over the weekend and copy it onto their floppy off of my computer and switch out the floppies in the express envelope with theirs. Slick, right?

I would come back in on Monday, make sure no one had anything else to go to Corporate, made sure the floppy was in there and send the packet off. Beautiful isn't it? So I never would have known any different.

I started to think, who would have wanted to get in there to change anything? Nothing made sense to me as none of the office staff would have anything to gain from it. Maybe the Sales Manager to show more sales? Not this guy, he was too lazy. Also he didn't have access to my password (that I knew of).

None of the salesmen because for one thing they didn't have access to my office and didn't have my password (at least not to my knowledge). But more sales was something that would affect their bonuses. No, I just don't think so. I couldn't imagine anyone else.

But after a long discussions with the Controller and the IT Manager we were able to put pieces together. One good clue was that we had a security guard in the building at night and you have to sign in and out each time you enter or leave the building. That's clue number one.

Also we used an identification card to get into the office just like the ones they use in hotels to get into your rooms. Our security system was able to identify the ID card and the employee it matched. That's clue number two.

Oh gosh, not another one of these….UGH!

While talking with the Controller I found out that the Site Vice President's monthly bonuses were directly affected through these increased sales numbers. And I mean these were <u>large</u> bonuses.

In addition, the VP was under pressure to increase sales by 20% that year. After even more intense research we found the individual doing it. (A big sigh), yup you guessed it, the Site Vice President that only stopped in once in a while was "falsifying" numbers so he could gain the bonuses and show an increase in sales. **Didn't I just go through this?** Another damn déjà vu.

Why do these people supposedly whom have professional backgrounds do this? Man I looked up to this guy. He was really nice. Don't these people know that faking numbers will ultimately be caught? Did they think this would go on forever? I cannot fathom a lot of this folks.

But again, I still read about these connivers every day. Just heard about a huge corporation in the news where the CEO fudged billions of dollars in profits for years. So you see…it never stops.

This guy threw away a perfectly beautiful career over this sabotage that took months to investigate and resolve.

What was he thinking?!! Ultimately he was let go and the corporate office decided that the whole site would shut down and consolidated with a southern suburb office site. I am positive that this incident had some impact on this decision.

They announced exactly that to all of us and they did indicate an option to transfer but again I just didn't want to move as I just purchased a home in a great suburb.

ONCE AGAIN… After 3 years with this company I was without a job. But at least we were forewarned a six weeks ahead to prepare.

If I didn't have any luck I wouldn't have anything at all. But I knew who to go to and how to network for gainful employment. By now I started feeling that someone higher up in the chain of life is exposing me to all this just so I can write about it. Has to be!

I already had my resume updated (remember to always do that when you take on a new position) just for situations like this one.

I got out my rolodex (that's my manual LinkedIn) and started contacting the local staffing agencies, started shopping through all the newspapers and networked with my business peers in the area.

One of the staffing agencies was able to help me acquire a secretarial position with a large software company that only provided hotel related software.

This was in one of the most beautiful buildings I've ever had the pleasure of working in. The building was 29 stories tall and this company was on the entire 4th floor.

There were computer IT folks everywhere in this building. My superior was a native from another country and set me up in a cubicle which was about three feet by three feet big and my back end was totally exposed to anyone walking by (and it was getting bigger).

I was basically in a hallway. But it seemed like it was going to be an interesting job per the description anyway and I really needed to work…so I happily settled in. They certainly paid well for the job I was doing so no complaints here.

The hours were great, all the office staff were supportive and I was so happy with the professionalism of everyone. Men in suits and women in dresses. And so many companies in this building alone. Great networking advantage. Ah-h-h finally!

I was located directly outside of my superior's office. The office manager was in a larger cubicle kiddy corner from me and did her best to arrange things and get me started with reading the employee handbook and showing me where office supplies were, etc.

Then she took me on a tour of the whole building showing me all the companies occupying it. In the lower level there was a complete retail area with a diner, dry cleaner, athletic room, barber shop/beauty salon and even childcare services-wow!

Oh-h-h....too good to be true. It was unfortunately. Within a few weeks I knew I was in trouble. **THERE WAS NO WORK TO BE HAD!**

My boss didn't give me any projects or assignments so I struggled endlessly asking for work. I'd inquire with the office manager or just anyone for anything to do on that entire floor.

While I was searching for work I soon realized that <u>no one</u> was busy and each clung to their own daily assignments or they wouldn't have anything to do either.

I made the determination that there were way too many staff for the work to be had. So many would be talking about their weekend or families at work because the just had nothing to do. No one seemed to care either.

I can't tell you how many times I dusted my desk just to look busy. I actually wore off the finish with as many times I had done that. I would purposely flip through files pretending to be auditing them. Man this was getting old. Why the heck was I hired anyway?

What a cluster of wasted time, energy and salaries. I did however have a very nice IT guy in a large office behind me. I'd go visit with him daily but knew that I couldn't continue bothering him.

When I would sit in this IT guy's office, his screen saver on his computer had a real scary skull flash on it. Within a minute it would change into a beautiful woman.

Later he told me that was his ex-wife (how cute – what an affectionate guy - NOT!!). After a few weeks of twiddling my thumbs, the office manager gave me the responsibility of backing up the receptionist while she went out to lunch. HOORAY! Something to look forward too!

One hour of feeling productive! Don't get me wrong the company paid me *extremely* well to do nothing and once a week our supervisor would take us out for lunch. It was absolutely terrific for anyone who enjoys doing nothing.

But over time that's not me and it was agonizing trying to keep busy. Faking 20 trips to the bath room was quickly fading as another thing to do. It just baffled me at how many people were doing this every single day. Thousands of salaries out the door. I just didn't "get it."

Other staff kept out just enough paperwork so if anyone stopped by they seemed to be doing a project. They all clung to what little work they had. So ridiculous. Beautiful pay, building and area, but I had to make a decision soon as I was going stir crazy.

I knew that the company would have to pay a hefty headhunter commission if I left before 90-days since I was hired through an agency so I worked (not worked actually) for four months before I told the office manager it wasn't going to work out.

She knew. I mean come on, be realistic…I can't sit at a desk and stare at a computer all day doing nothing. She didn't have much to do either. Besides my supervisor would have some of the oddest vapors spewing from his office.

Some made you gag! I later found out about his farting history from the other girls. Now remember, my desk was directly in outside his door which was the only exit direction for any vapor action.

I just keep getting luckier and luckier don't I? We started guessing the vapor to figure out what he had for lunch. Gotta find something to enlighten our day.

After I gave notice the office manager told me the only reason I was hired was because another supervisor got a secretary so this guy wanted one too. A-h-h-h-h, coveting and begetting are such nice words.

I felt bad for her as she knew it all along. It must be awful to interview for a bogus position and tell all those lies to get that person hired. Some of us do things because we don't think we have any other choice.

I think she liked me and wanted to be honest about it. Geez Louise folks! How could she hire someone on knowing that was the real reason? I somewhat felt sorry for her being placed in that position.

Truthfully I think she was just following orders from a higher up. Really nothing she could do about it. Well about five weeks before I gave that office manager notice, I knew I would need a job so I started sending resumes out prior to that.

Chapter IX

Through my diligence I was fortunate to gain a nice Senior Generalist role for a very established and strong paper converting manufacturer in a large suburb.

This company had plants in the South, Midwest and Europe. I didn't think I had a chance at it, but I was pleased to see I could still interview well. Finally a long founded, professional and solid company with a great reputation.

What a relief and there's still hope for an HR career……….it gets even better ladies and gentlemen…………………You do believe me don't you?

Okay, by now you know it doesn't so I'll start from the beginning with this job which I will term as the **worst** I had ever worked for.

Now remember I said "One" of the worst ones. There's even another bad job after this one as you read on. Isn't that great? So much to look forward to? That's why I'm writing this book with this title. I am truly blessed! (Huh?)

After I applied, I was fortunate to gain an interview. Wow, my first initial discussion was with the Vice President of HR. Such an honor. They are very serious if they have the VP of HR doing the interviews.

Well to start off and I'm sorry but this guy was extremely professional, in an expensive suit and very nice, but……he had an obvious hair piece on. It was off color and very crooked. Needless to say, I had a very difficult time concentrating on what he was saying because of it.

Unfortunately my serious and professional demeanor was quickly diminished after he sneezed and the darn hair piece moved halfway in front of his face!! Ugh!

Of course I was gracious enough to not laugh (boy was the hard to do-but I think I tinkled my panties). I let him know that he looked even better without it. Nice comeback, huh? Well a week later he called and I got the job! Yippee! Yahoo!

Whatever....

So I came in for my first day of work and the VP of HR spent some time with me to discuss my immediate responsibilities. Shortly after our discussion he took me where my office would be which was directly across from the Human Resources Manager's office which I later found out they hadn't one hired yet.

So I would be new and the soon to be new HR Manager would be arriving also. Kind of exciting if you think about it. A whole new HR Departmental staff starting. AND I found out I would be part of the interview process when they recruit this person. I was feeling mighty important now.

Well I walked into my new office and I noticed a massive amount of papers just lying everywhere on the floor in my soon to be office. Evidently these were individual employee's files of recent hires needing to be set up in folders and placed in filing cabinets. There was about twenty of them lying on the floor.

They had an HR Generalist before me but evidently they caught her making too many personal purchases on the company credit card. And yet another honest worker!

I couldn't wait to start! Really? Actually I really couldn't wait to get that mess cleaned up. The following Monday I started my new job. I opened the office door hoping the mess was gone, but the files were still there neatly stacked in their respective piles.

You literally could not walk on the floor without moving some files or stepping on them. The acting HR Supervisor was there to greet me and wish me "Good Luck" then shut my door and let me deal with it. Hey...could I get a cup of coffee first sir?!

This took me a whole week to get them off the floor and get them organized in files while handling day-to-day issues and learning payroll processing as well.

The current "acting" human resources manager was actually the production manager and he was going back into that role soon. He was such a nice person too. Sure hope they find one similar in personality. Tee-hee-hee. Come on guys...I'm still an optimist.

So the Corporate Vice President of Human Resources started the interview process for our human resources management replacement. So many new things happening. The days just flew by. I went from doing nothing to being overwhelmed with work. I did enjoy it so I was a happy camper.

This facility had three buildings all in the same block with about 200 staff. Mostly production and floor supervisory people.

The VP of human resources selected the temporary human resources manager, an engineer and myself to be involved in the human resources management selection process. I was deeply honored to be asked. To me that was very considerate of this VP of HR.

We would hop in the company car and periodically drive to the corporate headquarters about a half hour away to interview these chosen candidates. There were six candidates that were selected for the process and eventually we got it down to three finalists. Two men and one woman.

When I was alone with one of the final candidates (the female), I sat down in front of her, congratulated her on being one of the finalists and did some small chit-chat about the company. I noticed she wore a mini skirt, long earrings and was chewing gum. OH HELL NO!!

Okay, aren't the days of charming a male interviewer with miniskirts gone? Well this was the early 90's. Nope, I guess not. I'm one who doesn't take well with this type of interviewing garb. Especially for someone trying for a management role.

You would think a candidate would wear a suit or dress that was appropriate. Oh stop it, I'm not a fuddy duddy. But this was totally inappropriate. Chewing gum? Shut up! Bangle dangles on her wrists, chiming earrings...wait she looked like a band singer! A song comes to mind, "Oh Girls Just Wanna Have Fun!"

After getting over her garb, we began talking about the position again. Yah....she started to really open up now. She'd scoot closer to me and as she was chewing her gum profusely (snap, snap, pop) she opened her mouth and said, "Okay, I've gone through a couple of interviews now so tell me all the juicy shit that's going over there."

"What's really going on?" "Why are they looking for another HR Manager?" "What are the politics like over there?" "I think I'm on the low end of the pay scale for this job but I'm going to fight it." (It doesn't stop there folks...she keeps going).....

"I plan on working only 6-hours a day because of my personal obligations and you are doing all the work, ha-ha-ha-ha and ha." Ah-h-h yes, a perfect candidate...I immediately warmed up to her....**NOT!!**

Obviously, I knew right away that this person was not going to work out. So when the VP of Human Resources received everyone's feedback, we all came to the conclusion that she was in no way the right person and most of the handwritten concerns why were similar.

Since our opinion was so valued they **HIRED HER ANYWAY**!! Are you kidding me? Hooray for constructive feedback and a consensus! What the heck? There's your politics in action. Or maybe there's the mini-skirt and bangles in action. I just don't know.

I wasn't too concerned. She wasn't powerful in my books and certainly wouldn't be an effective person. I knew she would leave me alone to do everything and that was just fine and dandy with me!

Well a couple weeks later she started her new job and the new human resources manager did exactly what she stated. Got in at 9:30 am and left at 3:30 pm every day.

Within her first month she broke her finger walking her dog so she couldn't type anything or use the phone (so she claimed). So I got her coffee, did all her work (on top of mine), and answered her line for about 8 weeks.

Was I upset? Nah...this was great compared to all my previous jobs. She wasn't a threat or anything like that. She was worthless. But they were paying me very well and she left me alone so no complaints here.

She would have me come in her office just to gossip about some of the other managers. Her big issue was how much less she was making versus other managers.

This was quickly getting old folks. By now I had become a much tougher person and didn't like it when a manager acted that way. What a waste of my time. I've grown into maturity, but there will still be people in my life that can break you down and you learn of them as you read on.

After about four months of this crap I started telling her I couldn't visit anymore as I was getting further behind in paperwork. That went well actually as she didn't see a lot after that. I caught her onetime doing crossword puzzles. Underpaid? My ass she was.

Great News! All of the HR staff from the different sights were invited to attend some new payroll software training in a Southern state. I was excited to go and travel, see the other comrades and fly on the company expense.

Well my HR boss kept putting off getting her flight scheduled to the point of having me do it the day before. Her flight cost the company three times more than the rest because of her laziness. I couldn't believe she got on the same flight and was able to book a seat next to me. If I didn't have any luck at all-go figure.

This was very welcoming due to it being winter where I was and all. A Southern State was a good choice. And to learn something new is always great. I felt so important traveling with the company.

The Human Resources Manager sat next to me during the training as well. In fact, she was glued to me constantly. When the presenter started I would listen intently and took notes, she would lean over and start talking about the other human resources managers. This is so distracting lady!

Saying things like, "I wonder what they are getting for a salary." It was very difficult for me to concentrate with her constant interruptive and negative comments. Get a life woman!

> Pity Train to
> Loser-ville now
> departing on
> Track One.
> *Aaaall aboard!*

After a morning session of training we left to go into another room for lunch and when we came back into the classroom, I decided to sit next to another human resources generalist.

OH BOY! My HR Manager was livid that I did this and leered at me the whole time. During a break I explained to her that I never see any of the other associates and wanted to get to know them better. To myself I thought, "Who cares lady."

She said, "It doesn't matter, you're doing all this work anyway, I'm just here for the ride." I just cherished these positive reinforcing comments from my boss. Makes my heart warm and fuzzy all over yah know.

The company was working on a huge project which involved building a new facility in a Southern State. I worked with my supervisor a full year before I was asked by a higher up manager to consider transferring to this Southern State to start up a new manufacturing plant there.

He said that all the production and management staff felt I would be a good choice as I was a great "go to" person. I was honored to be considered.

Since I was recently divorced and a single parent, I felt a change would be good so I put in for the transfer. This ticked off my boss royally for two reasons; one she would need to replace me and two would she get someone who would do her beck and call? She didn't know how to do any of the generalist work (typical).

Another thing that ticked her off was she knew nothing about this new startup plant or that it was posted to internal candidates. That's because she NEVER WENT OUT ONTO THE FLOOR to read any updates. That was beneath her to walk the production floors.

I have to say though her boss should have kept her in the loop and he never did so okay I'll give her some slack for not knowing. But then again, maybe there was a reason he didn't say anything? Just saying.

Corporate should have also told her who from the company were being considered for a transfer so she could strategically prepare.

What am I saying? She won't do it…it'll fall in the laps of Corporate HR.

I had to present a 2-page letter indicating why I would be the best candidate for the transfer and submit my resume. About two weeks went by and low and behold I got the transfer. Maybe my luck was changing for the better. You would think so, but….yes that's right…let's all say it all together now; *"Just wait, it gets worse folks."* I'm thinking that might turn into a good song someday.

I've come to the resolution that a management title isn't all cracked up to what it should represent. I've known way too many that should never be managers. As you know my Human Resources Manager was extremely busy (NOT) and needed to find time in her busy schedule to perform my annual review. Besides she was only six plus months late with it…perfectly normal.

On the night before I was to leave I was working very late in the office to finish up loose ends. I stayed in the office until 10:30 pm that night.

As Gomer would say, "Surprise, Surprise, Surprise"…My boss, the Human Resources Manager was also there typing my review. Around 9:00 pm she hands me a brief case with a bow on it as a goodbye gift and does my review right then and there.

Okay folks**, its 9:00 pm for crying out loud!** I guess in her eyes it was a perfect time for this. Since it was late, she told me to basically read it, then sign it and then if I had any comments or questions to notify her as she was tired and needed to go home.

She then said, "Oh by the way, you'll get a 3% increase as well." We never did go through any of the subject matter or anything.

Nothing like feeling really appreciated. Yah gotta love her!

I really didn't care as I was so tired too. I later found out from our VP of HR that she was told to get it done before I leave or she would have to answer to him. Talk about the very last minute!

Anyway, I have found that late reviews or no reviews are very common these days. Did they back pay the increase? Oh hell no! That would be a total surprise indeed.

So the next day my U-Haul was packed. My daughter was now 16 and we were ready to take on this new and exciting career. My dad even flew down to help me so it became a nice family adventure!

How excited we were moving to a whole new State. I relocated relatively smoothly and this turned out to be a very lovely, pretty, low cost and friendly State by the way.

After I had gotten moved into this new town, I quickly became known in the area since we were a new company with a projected hire of 65 staff. This was a "Big Deal" to the community. I met a lot of nice people from the banks, chamber and small businesses.

Every time I would walk into another establishment I was greeted as if I were a queen. That's how valued this was to all the other businesses. It felt wonderful being treated so professionally.

Our company was building this brand new 25 million dollar facility and I was in charge of hiring, processing benefits, payrolls, onboarding and maintaining training documents on the production workforce.

We didn't have a building yet as it was being constructed so guess where all the engineers and managers worked each day? Yup…you guessed it…out of my new apartment.

Now mind you I have a daughter who was 16 at the time also living with me so this was very invasive to say the least. This arrangement went on for 3 weeks of working out of my home from 7:00 am to 7:00 pm.

Then after I gently mentioned this was getting more and more difficult on me and my daughter they at least had enough sense to get construction office trailers placed on the projected building site.

Not one time did anyone offer to reimburse me for the coffee, telephone line, condiments they ate, or part of my utilities they had utilized? I did get a handshake which meant so much to me (not really). More than not, people get taken advantage of. I'm such a sponge for everyone!

Yahoo…finally we had some privacy in our home! What a relief that was for us. About six months into the construction phase we had the initial building up, electricians were working on the electrical panels, cement trucks were pouring the parking lot and the building floors. People everywhere! Still much more to do yet.

The company eventually hired a new human resources manager to start. This gentleman's background was in recruitment at his previous role. He never touched on all the other functions such as benefits, law, disciplines, safety, etc.

He had no real knowledge of human resources policies and core competencies. His last title was "Talent Recruiter." I figure he's only done interviewing.

Since this would be new to him and more work for me I didn't mind as the excitement of the move and new facility was still occupying my mind.

Actually now that I think about it, the Controller did more of the human resources guidance for him. Both these guys were really nice people. So I was totally okay with it all.

Every 10 minutes the new HR Manager would ask me how to do something or where to find something. I was compassionate as he wasn't a bad guy really, but later would realize he was a "yes sir" man and not a person to challenge decisions which comes later.

It's not a good idea to hire someone who was only a recruiter and not exposed to all the other avenues in human resources. Especially when you expect them to manage it.

I remember him sitting in front of his computer and finally coming out to ask me how to access his email. I think he was conscious of the fact that he was leaning on me for help quite a bit but I never conveyed it was a burden.

He did not know how to attach files or anything. I felt sorry for him to tell you the truth. So I wanted to really help him. He was a nice guy.

For me to save time and effort I decided to show him more than just that. I trained him on all our software programs and policies.

I was very surprised that the company hired him. Normally they would usually hire assertive or more confident people and this person was very shy, introvert and to himself. Not like the other management staff at all. But as you read on, I finally figured out why they hired this "yes sir" kind of fella.

Another month went by and we were introduced to the newly hired Plant Manager. He seemed like a jovial fella.

OMG! Was I ever wrong! This is where the "job from hell" starts.

And I mean this was…oh just read and you'll see.

This guy was a 20-year military man and ran his office in that fashion. Some of the language that came out of his mouth was shocking. And I mean shocking!

Well I was amazed that he had enough sense to recognize that the construction trailers were cumbersome so he was able to rent an office building on a short term lease for the engineers and office staff. A real office building with toilets. Such a change from out houses.

No more buzzing sounds from horseflies under my ass while I'm taking a whiz. And the ambiance was unbelievable. Toilet treatment and poop! Great aroma combination. Like peppermint and a fart.

It became very busy with engineers and contractors coming and going. All kinds of building construction taking place. During that time I started to notice that the plant manager and the secretary/receptionist would leave the office building very often together for long periods of time and I mean hours each day.

She eventually told me that he was house hunting for his family that still lived in out-of-state and took her along for a second opinion. I asked her how she felt about all that and she said she wasn't comfortable but it was if he was giving a direct order or else.

First off he's her boss and secondly what does her opinion have to do with him buying a home? Should that be something his wife should be involved in? I know, stay out of it.

I could tell she was feeling mighty guilty of it and told me on several occasions how uncomfortable he made her feel. I asked her to give me specifics and she said he would say things like how pretty her hair was that day or the jewelry she was wearing.

Or that she was losing weight and looking sexy. HUH?!! She later confessed that she told him she was getting behind in work and shouldn't be accompanying him on these trips.

She said he then threatened her with her job if she didn't accompany him on these outings. She was only 28 and felt trapped. Are you kidding me? Another jerk boss? No way!

"You can't hurt his feelings — at least *pretend* to eat it."

They would also stop at restaurants and he insisted she have wine with their meals as she would come back into the office very tired and worn out. Wine in the middle of the work day? It's not the 80's anymore fella! The poor girl.

This was her first professional job and another a-hole has to ruin the image for her. She's going to think that all jobs are like this.

Now they would be gone anywhere from 1-5 hours daily for over 3 months so I ended up doing a lot of her work. Again, I really didn't mind as we weren't that busy yet.

She felt she couldn't get out of it as he was so forceful and demanding and I knew he was so I didn't blame her for a lot of it. I kept telling her that as I could tell she really needed a friend.

Well another training session was scheduled at that same place in the South. Since we already lived in this Southern state we were able to drive there.

I was hoping to go with someone I could relate too, but that was an impossible request. This time all the engineers and office staff needed to attend the conference. That was about 14 people total. It was some marketing thing with status updates on the company.

Now the Plant Manager thought it would be a great idea to rent an extended van and economically drive all of us there. Are you kidding me? All 14 of us together on a 2 hour drive? No way.

Well fortunately 2 were at the corporate office and would be flying to the conference from there so that left 12 of us. Now the van only holds 12 seats. How would he have gotten 14 in there in the first place? Geez Louise.

The 12 of us all squeezed into this van. Very uncomfortable for a 2-hour ride as some brought briefcases and items to work on during the ride. But the plant manager insisted and you know that when he's insisting you jump. This conference was from 10:00 am to 3:00 pm that day.

Well guess what! We didn't get back until 11:00 pm because on the way back from the conference, the Plant Manager wanted to look at homes and then later go out to a bar somewhere. We had no choice as he was our ride.

Four engineers were so upset that they contacted their spouses to pick them up just so they didn't have to go. There were six of us left in this van and most of us also protested stating our children were home alone and some had a school event they needed to attend and he said he didn't care, so we were stuck. What a super nice guy he was.

I know we were all adults but it was the way he said it and his body language that put fear in us. None of us felt we could do anything about it as he could make us lose our jobs. That's the way it was back then.

Sounds like the marriage I was in. Funny thing (not really) is we drove around so much that we **ran out of gas** on one of the highways. Can you believe it?! SH#T! What was this guy thinking?

We were only one mile from the next exit so three of us (yes, including me) ended up pushing this van while in neutral to the next exit and roll into a gas station very late at night. Nothing but adventures, adventures, adventures.

Now the Plant Manager sat in the driver's seat smoking a cigar and yelling out the window "mush you doggies" like he was on vacation. He looked like WC Fields in that position. I grew more and more to dislike him.

I knew it was my job to protect the staff and company, throughout all these incidences, I would talk about them with the Plant Human Resources Manager. You remember him?

The "yes sir" man. He couldn't do anything, but I had to go to him first! He would sympathize with me but just told me to buck up and bear it. You betcha! Thank you for your support.

Oh Heck…is this where I start to think about looking for another job again? Oh Hell no! I liked this company and job. I was now here 2+ years and I can deal with this stinker (yah think?). I was getting tougher all the time. I can get through this little inconvenience. (Have I talked myself up enough yet)?

A week later we finally got our computers up and running in this new temporary office. It was decided to have us independently process payrolls so we were doing parallel payrolls at the new office with corporates payrolls before we were able to do our own independently. Just to make sure they come out error free. You don't want to mess with anyone's paycheck.

While doing these payrolls mistakes were made with coding or language to communicate it to the payroll department or computers. This was from the corporate setup end-not ours. This is why you run parallel payrolls until all the quirks are worked out.

Well during one of our morning meetings our obviously infuriated Plant Manager announced in front of all the Engineers and office staff that the reason the payrolls were taking so long to be run independently and continue to be wrong was because I was totally incompetent.

Everyone in that meeting turned their eyes on me. Of course mine were bugged out too with this statement. What a horrible thing to say in front of everyone. This was not due to my inabilities, it was a programming problem connecting information from Corporate to us.

And he went on and on insulting my integrity. He then stated that he was taking payroll processing away from me and it would now be taken over by the Controller.

The staff started moving their heads down as to be in prayer. I just sat there embarrassed and infuriated. Wasn't worth my time to explain the root cause.

The girls in the office were so supportive but I knew they were uncomfortable at the moment. They hung their heads low too as not to look at me. I'm so tired of this….my eyes just dropped at this guy's audacity. I'm sitting in a room full of staff too scared to say anything. So sad actually.

After the meeting some of the staff came to my side to comfort me, but I was at a point of really not caring anymore as I knew who it was coming from.

As I've grown in human resources and now becoming seasoned in this business, I've discovered a lot more stupidity out there and became more convinced at just how good I had become. I've never faltered my integrity or competence. And that folks is your foundation. It's not you….it's them!

I have found that people in high powers more often than not take that power to their heads. It excites them to use it at the cost of others. And believe it or not, some do it because they actually have no clue and it makes them look knowledgeable.

I've been a Director before and I can say that there's greater rewards for those who are in control of themselves and not others. Let me get off my soapbox for now. Anyway….

The payrolls continued to be wrong even when the Controller was in charge of it. Imagine that-really? A week later the corporate payroll manager finally flew out to do some additional fixes and training with the Controller, myself and the secretary as backup. The corporate payroll manager was an awesome dude! So friendly, supportive and pretty much a guru of payroll systems.

While training, the Plant Manager came up to us where we were sitting and loudly exclaimed how unsophisticated this payroll system was and that we were all incompetent for even using it. Everyone in that office just stared at him.

It was so neat to finally have someone from corporate experience this wonderful plant manager of ours-NOT! The plant HR manager came in right after and apologized to the payroll manager. Not to us-his staff, just the payroll manager.

After he left the corporate payroll manager turned to me and stated "boy, he's a nice guy isn't he?" Of course he was being sarcastic. I told him. "You have no idea" and to try working with that every day.

But it saddened me that my boss didn't defend us. I mean this was the corporate payroll manager for heaven's sake. Oh, I forgot...how could be due to the fact that this poor guy was glued to the Plant Manager's behind.

Sorry, didn't mean to be rude but it's true. All of us were adults and not one of us did anything. Just kept taking it. What do you call that? Oh yeah, co-dependents.

Well I was secretly doing something about it by updating my resume and putting some feelers out there just in case. It only takes one bad leader to screw up a whole company. I've seen it way too many times.

Well about an hour after that nice comment the Plant Manager came back in and said he needed to have the secretary leave with him on an errand. She had to be taken away from cross-training and was gone the rest of the day, returning only to pick up her car which ended up being around 6:00 pm.

I informed the payroll manager that this is a regular incident three to four times a week and not just her but other Engineers or staff get forced to go with him outside.

I told him about the time we went to training in another town and ended up pushing an empty van to a gas station all hours of the night. This corporate payroll manager's eyes were huge in just complete shock!

In a way, I was doing this as a chance he might say something to someone in Corporate. I could only hope. Well he left and we were finally able to do payrolls on our own.

Oh boy…it's getting bad now. Arrggg! Waaaaaaa! Just shoot me now!

The following week it was such a nice day that a bunch of us office girls were having lunch together outside the building on the picnic table and the Plant Manager walked up to us with all smiles. He then asked us to open our hands.

He said he wanted to show us a neat trick. He was rather jolly and we were hooked. He then took the white filter from cigarettes and put one in each of our hand and proceeded to pour a liquid of some sorts in our hands and asked us to shake it.

Then he instructed us to open our hands and to our shock the material inside looked exactly like male semen. He started laughing profusely holding his stomach and asked us what we thought that was and walked away.

We just sat there in shock of it all holding our hands out as if we were beggars. (Oh the pain of all this)…

Now all of us were professional ladies and two sitting with us were engineers. What was this guy thinking?! Time goes by.......

About a few months earlier it had been announced that we had a new President of the company. Then about a month later we were 60% completed with the construction of the new facility.

The Plant Manager instructed (all the engineers and myself) to work on and provide a presentation to this new President of the company who was flying out from the corporate headquarters in a week.

This was going to be a typical "dog and pony show" viewing the progress of the plant construction and meet any new staff. I was appreciative of being asked to help.

The Plant Manager wanted us to develop a PowerPoint presentation so he decided at the last minute to call a mandatory meeting to go over the topics. This meeting started at 4:00 pm on Friday evening. We all had to stay in, <u>none could leave the building</u>.

He would not allow us to take more than one restroom break nor call our families that we were still at work. If someone was in the washroom more than three minutes, he would run over and pound on the stall door. SICK, MENTAL MAN!

Seriously folks, he was way out there. More disturbing fearful thoughts of this boss started to infiltrate my brain. Something that's gone beyond the scope of controlling behavior.

This meeting ultimately ended at 1:00 am. Yes, you heard me right…**1:00 AM!**

I got home and my daughter who was 16 at the time was crying hysterically, frightened that I had been in an accident and she had no way of contacting me.

I had to explain to her that I could not call, but how do you do that? At her age she wouldn't think a boss would be so horrible. She thought I didn't care about her anymore.

I held her all night and told her no matter what that this would never happen again! I DESPISE that S.O.B. for putting my kid in that situation!

I needed to go back in late that night to formulate what needed to be done. I decided to take her with me and she could use the computer to do stuff on it.

She was a little apprehensive for fear of seeing him there. I told her not to worry that I would be right there with her and I wasn't going to let the S.O.B. mess our day up no matter what the cost.

I felt terrible telling her that. What kind message was I sending her? Will this be her idea of a normal office job? Fortunately the Plant Manager wasn't there that weekend so I was able to have a very nice and productive day with my daughter. We had to get this presentation done.

So that meant the next two days I ended up working until 4:00 – 6:00 AM with two engineers (yes that was Saturday and Sunday). They did the technical data and I got it into a readable and professional PowerPoint Presentation.

Luckily my daughter could come those days too so she wasn't left alone and brought her sleeping bag. At least she wasn't afraid anymore.

I know at 16 she should be a little more independent and grown up. But what you have to understand is she didn't have a dad and more than 70% of the time her mom wasn't there either due to working. I hated that part of our life.

She was a "clingy" and "needy" kind of girl which didn't bother me. I totally understood why and did everything I could to give her what she needed which was me being with her.

I also had the job of contacting the country club to arrange a room for all this to happen, make catering, hotel and transportation arrangements. Me under pressure? Nah, not at all…(I'm being sarcastic yah know).

The next business morning was Monday and we left the office at 6:00 am Monday morning after working all night on it. **IT WAS**

DONE! We had to be at the Country Club and Conference Center to do this presentation by 8:30 AM so no sleep was to be had. I went home and took a shower, fully refreshed at least on the outside and returned to the country club.

The new President and many other corporate VP heads were in attendance. Probably about 50 people total so it was a big deal. I was sitting at one of the tables directly across all these high officials unfortunately next to the Plant Manager.

Now here is where I could use a stiff drink or even a bullet screaming by. I despised being near him.

He would just smile and suck up to all the higher ups. I had to do initial introductions before the presentation.

Then all of a sudden, the Plant Manager jumped up next to me at the podium, grabbed my notes and began giving the introductory speech. I just stood there in awe of this man.

What kind of animal is this? I stayed right there next to him mostly due to embarrassment. Then he did it! He opened his damn mouth and personally thanked the two engineers for sacrificing their personal time getting this done. Applause came next as the two engineers stood up.

There was not one mention of **me** working the whole time with these guys.

UGH....I hung my head low in despair by this. I guess all my efforts and sacrificed time were meaningless. I should have known he would do this. What a Sh@t he was. We stepped down and went back to our seats.

I wanted to get outside for some air but the Plant Manager leered at me when I stood up so I sat back down. When the speeches and presentations were over as everyone started to disperse I was finally able to get up to take a break outside as I was ready to burst into tears.

As I got up, the Plant Manager asked me in front of everyone where I was going and I said that I need to use the washroom and he said "that's a lame excuse" and said how rude I was for leaving at that time and not mingling with the higher ups.

I didn't care and just blurted it out in front of everyone, "If you don't let me go, I'll pee my pants right now, is that what you want?" and walked out. His eyes were wide open with anger over my arrogance! I just didn't care. **BACK AT YAH BUD!**

About 5 minutes later I returned after refreshing myself and feeling a bit better. On a nice note, the President came over to me to thank me for putting this event together and shook my hand. Very refreshing.

Even one of the engineers I worked with all weekend came over to shake my hand and he told me that he mentioned to the higher ups that I also sacrificed my time. I was grateful to him for that but it was mute by then.

Everyone went into another room to have lunch. I sat at one of the tables and the Plant Manager purposely sat next to me-again? Geez Louise! He mumbled that I never going to refuse his orders again and I made him look like a fool. What is it with this guy?

I'll bet he was a perfect military torture person. That's it! Had to be. Hey…maybe I should turn the gun on him? After he said that to me, I LOUDLY and I mean loudly replied, "And for my punishment, what will that be this time?" "Working until 2:00 am?" "Looking for homes with you or maybe termination?"

Bring it on buddy ole pal! The whole room went quiet. I had it! Nothing could be worse than this. He's just a man for heaven's sake, not the almighty.

Now whatever that meant I didn't care. I was hoping he would do something inappropriate right then and there in front of all those witnesses, but no, he was smarter than that.

He just laughed and said "We joke around like this all the time." Even grabbed my shoulders and shook them as if we were comrades. Sickening. But I feared my dues were soon forthcoming for that little scene.

Some of the engineers met me out in the parking lot and said I should talk to the corporate headquarters about what was going on and I was feeling numb so I really wasn't up to it just then. I need rest right now. What? Why didn't they? Why is it always me, me and me to fix all this?

But later I thought to myself, why would they say that? Maybe they thought I would be believable and credible. But again, it's me against a world of business politics and managers who do not want to deal with these types of things. And yes, unfortunately being a "WOMAN" back then was regarded as "she's not important so her thoughts mean squat."

Well I was very surprised that nothing happened to me after that. But it was a constant miserable time as a couple more months passed.

He gave me stupid assignments that amounted to nothing. No productive work. Pretty much the norm, the Plant Manager and secretary were once again out a lot constantly looking for houses.

Oh, and by the way, his wife was now coming up a lot too with their little 1-year old daughter. I found out his wife used to be his secretary and he ended up getting her pregnant and ultimately they got married.

Here's how nice I am, I babysat their child so they could enjoy their weekends together (am I a Saint or what?). This was his 5th wife to be exact now.

About a 15 year age difference I think. I could tell there was stress in their marriage. Who wouldn't be with that? She was a hard looking woman. She's taken on a lot of abuse over a period of time.

You could see she was a very unhappy lady. I think she and I would have been good friends if it wasn't for that one guy she was hooked up with.

His wife was just as formidable and strong as he was. She had gotten hard from his demeanor and she would tell me stuff like, if anything happened to their marriage, their home in another state was in her name only and so on.

This woman didn't know me but she would open up to me as if I were her best friend. That just tells me how badly she needed to talk with someone.

I felt bad for her but I really didn't care. I actually got to like her quite a bit and just wondered how she first could have worked for a guy like that let alone marry the S.O.B?

Plant construction was now 70% complete at this time. We still didn't have floors in the building so it was rock and dirt, but the main structure was intact and they were finalizing all the electrical and plumbing additions.

It was awesome seeing this thing come together. Man there were some huge pieces of equipment inside. Hard hat workers everywhere.

The Plant Manager came in one day and wanted to celebrate being 70% complete by bringing employee families and their children at the work site to see it. Similar to an "Open House."

I **immediately** protested and stated this was not recommended as we were still in construction phase meaning all that enter would need hard hats, safety glasses and steel toe shoes. There were regulations to follow on a construction site.

For crying out loud we still had overhead cranes inside this building and no working toilets. It was not a safe area for outside guests' especially little children running around. Are you kidding me?

He again said, "I don't care, I'm the boss of this operation and I want them to come out and bring the kids."

BRING THE KIDS?! Sure we have cranes, forklifts, holes, unprotected wiring and many other obstructive objects where they could get hurt on. Why not?! I again protested stating that this was such a liability for us.

He then stated he also wanted food and beer catered in. Holy Cow! What?!! Is he insane? (Well we already knew this). **BEER** at a business construction site?

This whole thing was getting ludicrous and seemed like an impossible situation, but this was so serious a situation that I didn't care if I lost my job at this point.

This wasn't about me, but about the safety of strangers, children and the Company's liability. For about two weeks I didn't hear anything of it and was hoping he dropped it.

Well he didn't…one day a production employee walked up to me and said he needed petty cash and was instructed by the Plant Manager to purchase 6 cases of beer for this Open House event the upcoming Saturday.

I immediately went to my boss, the Human Resources Manager to express my strong case of not doing this and obviously why. He agreed with me but said he wasn't sure if he could convince the Plant Manager. This guy has a stronghold on all of us. **ENOUGH!**

During a site meeting in a room near my cubicle I overheard my HR boss tell the Plant Manager of his concern with the open house plans (why didn't the he bring this up before is beyond me).

After he stated that the Plant Manager screams at the top of his lungs out to the office, "I've had it with her, she came to you with this didn't she?" "I'm going to fire her ass if she doesn't do this."

Obviously he was talking about me and all in that office heard this as all eyes were on me when I stepped into the break room. Nope, I didn't hear my boss say "no, this is MY concern not hers." Taking responsibility is not his nature.

I was so overwhelmed with the constant verbal abuse, tired of working long hours and weekends, of not seeing my child, I had to just flat out leave!

It was over....no more for me. 4 years with this company giving up so much to get this place running. I was a complete emotional wreck.

As I walked out of the office into the parking lot I started to cry uncontrollably (you can only take so much yah know). Some of the engineers were walking in the building at the same time and kept saying, "Are you okay?" I just shook my head and kept crying as I walked to my car. There was no way I was in any condition to talk just then.

The secretary saw this and knew I was too shaky to drive so she ran after me in the parking lot and hugged me. She felt compassionate to drive me home.

We talked on the way home and she also was at her wits end. She encouraged me to do what I felt was right because she was too afraid too. She told me that a lot of people in the office would back me up.

Geez, no one ever defended me earlier so why would I think they would now? She even thought she would be in trouble for driving me home. She's right! If he finds out, she's in do-do land.

She begged me to say something to the Vice President of Human Resources. She hugged me as I got out of her car and looked at me with such despair and fear. I felt so sad about all of this. For everyone. Well if I had to be the martyr then so be it. How can these people exist? Why can't other higher ups see any of this?!

As I sat in my living room calming down, collecting my thoughts and getting my head right. I then decided it was truly time to make that phone call. I just couldn't risk these hazardous conditions for the public and also reflected on all the previous crap so I called the corporate Vice President of Human Resources.

I told his secretary it was an emergency so I would get him right away. I was shaking so bad. The VP of HR answered the phone right away. I took a huge deep breath and then went into the details of telling him what was going on.

From the beginning to now. He never interrupted me and was so quiet on the other end. I kept say, "Are you there?" and he would indicate yes, just shocked and urged me to continue.

I indicated to him that I would most likely fired for refusing to help with the open house. I also told him that everyone in that office has been affected and have urged me to be the person who made the call.

Our conversation went on for over two hours. He then asked me to email him with all the details. I told him it would take me more than a day to get this to him and he said he was going fly out right away and would be here in a few days, but to have as much as possible for him as quickly as possible.

The Corporate VP of Human Resources reassured me that I was not fired and thanked me for protecting the company. He stated that I should take the next two days off (it was Monday and Tuesday of the week) and he'll authorize it and notify my boss who is the Site HR Manager.

I hung up that phone and all of a sudden I felt this HUGE weight lift off of me. A VP actually listened to me for 2-hours. I must have made sense or he would have stopped me.

I was curious how that was going to pan out with the VP of HR calling the site HR to tell them I'm going to be off a couple of days?

You know there will be obvious questions and I asked the VP of HR just that. He told me that's all I'm going to tell them and they can make their own conclusions. THIS was going to interesting.

It must have been right after he got off of the phone with me that he notified my site boss who immediately called me to ask why would the VP of HR would be reporting my absence?

Well this didn't sit well with my site manager and he immediately told the Plant Manager. I know this because some engineers called me to tell me what happened.

They both went all over to everyone in the office inquiring with everyone there if I had said anything to them. Oh...and of course he would threaten the staff if they held back any information he should know about. Yeah, that's right, bury yourself in deeper dude!

It doesn't take much to figure out the assumption that I was the whistle blower and they started to plan whatever they needed to plan.

The Plant Manager had the secretary shred some documentation, had the plant straightened up and held an emergency meeting telling all staff to "keep their mouths shut." Yah Pal...more threats! Keep digging that deeper and deeper and I'm going to throw away the shovel!

The VP of HR then called me back and said he would be coming out Thursday to do a full research of what I told him. He told me to report to work every day as usual the following Wednesday and not say anything to anyone, just do my job. He also thanked me again and told me he supported me 100%. Gosh I felt so good by then.

He said that if the Plant Manager or HR Manager questioned me, to tell them I've been instructed to report to the VP of HR going forward and that all communications go through him.

I have to tell you folks, even though this wasn't over, somehow I felt very relieved in some way. I was confident the VP of HR had my back and that this was going to get fixed. I slept so well that night. (A massive sigh).

When I got to work, no one spoke to me and everyone except a few engineers avoided me. I know why it was this way and I felt somewhat back in charge of myself. I knew the Plant Manager probably threatened them if they were seen communicating with me.

I took that as an opportunity to just to do what I was hired to do. I would look at the secretary and she would smile but only for a very short time for fear of being caught favoring me. I was so relieved with no more crap. I didn't care if they let me go as I had my integrity and confidence back.

No one in their right mind would stay and it's beyond me why I or others did. We are so co-dependent with any bad relationships whether it's personal or professional. We have to get over that "fear of losing your job" syndrome as there are plenty out there if you have skills.

I was very pro-active though and started sending out my resume in the area. I had some longevity with the company and a great HR background so finding a position wouldn't be too difficult, at least that was my take on it.

A discussion from Corporate must have taken place as shortly after a morning staff meeting the Plant Manager announced we would be changing our Open House celebration to a local bar/restaurant that will also cater food for us. After he announced this he walked away very quiet. Never raised his voice. Almost as if he was defeated.

Now this was the day before the event and we had not had time to get anything arranged. No decorations, no invites, not even reserving the room, no nothing!

So I had to really hit the pavement to get all of this completed, but with perseverance I managed to get it all done. "Git er done!"

On Saturday I went to this bar early to decorate one of the large rooms for this event and the Plant Manager walked in and later, paused and just stared at me. Man, talk about feeling uncomfortable! I was by myself and suddenly felt like a trapped animal in a cage with nowhere to escape. He walked over to me and he had this look of defeat on him.

I sensed pity on him as admitting I was right must have been very difficult for someone with an ego as his. He then verbally told me that my decision was the right one about not having it at the construction site and just walked away.

I didn't have to say anything. All of a sudden I had to sit down as I felt woozy for a second. Maybe it's because he and I were alone, or maybe what may have come out of his mouth. I didn't know how to handle that at all but glad it was short and sweet.

Out of 100 staff only about 25 people showed up for the event and maybe 6 had spouses with them. Most of them were from the production floor and maybe 3 managers.

I only saw a couple of engineers and the secretary of course. No one could bring a child to the bar either so not very many staff were there. Kind of a sad time really.

It was a somber and quiet time to say the least. I don't think anyone was comfortable or enjoyed themselves. I considered it a disaster, not a celebration.

Hardly any of the food was eaten. No one was drinking or socializing. Maybe it was because he was there. About an hour later the Plant Manager announced he had to get home and left.

Once he left, everyone went to the bar, then started playing pool and mingling. Chitter Chatter everywhere. Another hour went by and I made arrangements with the bar owner for cleanup so I could go home too. I was exhausted!

Some time went by and I eventually found out in the next two weeks that I wasn't the only one who has contacted Corporate over the Plant manager's management style as the VP of Human Resources did fly over and asked several other staff to document everything that has been going on since day one.

Just as he said the big guy and I mean the Vice President of Operations flew in a few weeks later to talk to me and others personally. Naturally I was nervous but forthright in thought as well. He was the next in command to the President of the company.

I had to maintain nothing but the facts of what was going on.

Not to take up his time I gave him a short summary of key incidents. He then gave me his private laptop to document everything I told him and anything else. WOW! His own personal laptop!

He asked me to complete it by the end of the evening – not in great detail, but point out as many incidents as possible which took me until 2:00 am to finish but this was very important to me. The fact that I was finally being supported by such higher ups was phenomenal.

There was so much that my fingers got numb typing. After I finished and turned in my information the next day to the VP of Operations, some of the staff decided to get together to talk about it that evening at a local establishment.

We were the people who were chosen to inform upper management of these horrendous situations. Two were key engineers, one from the production floor and myself.

I found out later that this same Plant Manager threatened an engineer with his life if some dealings were revealed. This is like a TV action movie (but more on the drama side). Can you believe this? Where am I?

Eventually all of us "whistle blowers" met at a restaurant. I think we did this to have some type of support amongst ourselves as we all felt alone with all this mess.

I wish I would have known this earlier. We could have supported each other throughout this ordeal, but none of us knew about each other's communications.

I didn't say much as I feared a spy might be amongst us and this was pretty much a private situation. I had gotten so paranoid by now with all of this. I more or less just stayed quiet and nodded my head once in a while...who could be trusted?

What am I talking about? The Plant Manager did all this in public so there probably wasn't one staff member who didn't know all these bad things going on. But again, the risk taking was over and none of us knew what the other knew so when we finally did talk it all came together.

For about four weeks after all this the Plant Manager acted very quiet around us most of the time. Once in a while he would tell a joke or two to some of the Engineers but he stayed away from the gals.

He no longer left for long periods of time nor did he take the secretary out with him anymore. No one was saying anything and it became stagnant, kind of spooky actually.

I was walking behind one of the gal's cubicle and noticed she was typing the termination letter for this Plant Manager. I sat next to her and as we talked I turned a little to read the letter and I was shocked!

Guess what? This S.O.B. was getting a year's severance. WTF?! After all he did and all the misery he put this staff through? He gets a year's pay? Once again it pays to be bad.

Eventually that fall this plant manager was ultimately terminated and the Site Human Resources Manager was reprimanded for not handling this appropriately nor supporting me or other staff while this was going on after being told repeatedly.

I did discover that the payroll manager from corporate also mentioned the run in he had with this guy which only supported it even more.

I don't think Corporate had gotten a real feeling on how much control this guy had on all of us. This was such a liability to the company. I felt I would never meet a boss like that again.

(A moment of silence please). H-m-m-m-m-m. Now I know as you are reading this you are already saying, nah...she's going to have another boss like this. **Oh Really?**

You would think this was one of the worse? Okay, you guessed it folks. **Boy was I ever wrong.** I'll be mentioning another sick situation later on in the book. First I have to absorb some antacids as while I'm typing this my stomach is starting to react to it all. Just a minute……….

Okay, I'm back. Needless to say that experience also ended my working relationship with the Site Human Resources Manager as he felt betrayed by me for telling the VP of HR he didn't back any of our concerns up. He wouldn't come near me for weeks.

I think he was actually ashamed and embarrassed that an employee took charge. Was that what it was? Taking charge or just giving up is how it felt to me. But I understood the other side working for that man.

With all that had happened in my previous roles I had gotten a sense of "so what?" attitude as long as I knew my actions were morally and ethically right. I the only thing I could do.

It was never my intention to throw my immediate supervisor under the bus and I actually defended him by telling the VP of Human Resources that it was out of everyone's control.

But evidently they didn't see it that way. He should have been more assertive and be the one notifying them and not an employee. And they are right.

I could not let this Plant Manager keep destroying lives daily. Gosh my heart isn't into this anymore. Just shoot me now!

After this Plant Manager was removed I later found out that this same Plant Manager was terminated from his three previous Companies as well and they were very reputable firms. I think a lot of information opened up once he was gone. Don't we do background checks on people? Obviously not.

When all of this was happening before he was terminated the Plant Manager's wife stopped in to see me a couple of times and knew something was up. She would state to me, "I hope he's not getting fired again."

I should have gotten a clue then. What?! I later asked her what that statement meant and she told me that some staff at another company complained about his management style and got him fired. Holy Cow! This is like a broken record over and over again.

Wow! Obviously she's used to this. She then said she hated him and had a prenuptial with him. A little too much information lady. See he's been married four times before and I believe had 5 daughters. Wife number 5 wasn't taking any chances.

It just baffles me that this plant manager made so many threats to so many people and not one person came forward? Not a one people! This man had such a strong overbearing presence to bring down nineteen full grown professional adults.

I know the impact this had on everyone but no one sued the company over it either and that could easily have happened. I could have sued and I think that's why they treated me so well during all this.

That's not what happens today, you can have an employee sue over just about anything. That's another HR nightmare chapter folks.

To me resolving this issue came way too late though. The office would be eerily quiet and we acted like lost zombies. It was such a strong impact on all of us that the healing process was somewhat numbing. It was an uncanny feeling.

That was a long chapter wasn't it?

Chapter X

I was 43 then but felt more like 60 years old during all this turmoil and within all this havoc I had also started dating one of the project engineers with the company but from another State.

He actually resided in the Midwest and flew back and forth consulting for this new construction project. We became heavily involved and it soon blossomed into a full blown romance. I'm not sure if he knew anything of the goings on but later he indicated that he did.

Approximately six months later the company overall went through a massive layoff and I was included in the selection process along with 40 other staff throughout three States.

Deep down inside I feel I was included because I stood up for what was right and they had some fear of my convictions for the future. Or maybe not, but most of those from my plant that were laid off were very vocal people.

Several were part of the information gathering investigation that got that Plant Manager removed. You had to believe that some of this impacted a large portion of who were to be laid off.

I was surprised that the site HR Manager was still there though. Office politics play such a strong part in corporations. It wasn't hard to figure out. That will change later.

Whistle blowers are never protected and actually feared of their strength and ability to open up. But in the end, I am extremely thankful it happened as for one thing, the whole thing was exhausting and change was needed.

And I received so many "Thanks" from engineering spouses, workers over this whole thing. Even some community members thanked me. Geez this guy impacted everything!

Secondly, it opened my doors to much better career choices (at the time). I'll be eating those words very soon when you read on. Oh Really? Can it be? Okay, altogether now, repeat after me,

"Oh Hell Yah It Can!"

Back to the layoff....

Part of the layoff process was that the company would pay for a consultant to assist us with interviewing, resume creation and job searches. We were credited with a week's worth of service. About nine of us would meet at the local college to participate in this.

This consultant was the actual owner of the business and flew in from another State to personally perform this training. While this was going on, I didn't waste any time and I began my job searches the moment of the layoff.

Gosh, I'm having a brain flarp. I have to tell you about an interview I had that was for a Human Resources Management position. The company sounded really neat and the drive wasn't bad at all. I brought my daughter along for the ride and while she waited in the car I went to the interview.

I met this gal who had the title of Vice President of Human Resources. We went to the small conference room and she started to talk about……her. I learned about her management style, where she lived, what she likes to do in her spare time and what kind of car she drives...for THREE HOURS FOLKS! Not one time did she ask me about my experience or skills?   Man was my butt sore sitting there so long.

She didn't elaborate on the job opening itself or the company's history. She looked at her watch and said we have talked more than expected. WE? Who we? You lady.

She then shook my hand and said she'd be in touch. I never did hear anything back from her. Probably one of the worst interviews I've ever had. My poor kid was sitting in that car for 3-hours. I put her through so much sometimes.

As promised I took her shopping and out to dinner as I felt bad having her wait so long but I didn't expect to go through something like that. Am I being optimistic again? I don't want to enter into interviews or jobs wondering how crazy they may be. I want to keep thinking there's a professional entity out there. Just has to be.

While I was job searching and taking advantage of this independent consultant that the previous company paid for. I also got to know the consultant quite well. Fortunately for me within a few days I was able to acquire a business office management position with a historical museum very close to previous job.

I was thrilled, imagine me working in a historical museum. I would go to the consultant's class happier than a lark, but I didn't want to gloat too much with all the others still getting used to their situation and was fearful of not finding work. But I stood up and made the announcement that I found a job, wished everyone else the very best and left.

What a neat job folks. This was a house built in 1926. House, I mean mansion with 60 foot ceilings. Had a full library, full wall fireplace and a dining room that could fit 30 guests. Encased in glass was a $75.00 check from George Washington. Had decorations from 600 B.C. This was an awesome place!

12 bedrooms with 12 bathrooms. Each room was themed from wherever the owners traveled. One room was decorated in Jade so it was called the oriental room, another was small tea tables, white linens and shear drapes. This was known as the English room and so on.

The servant's quarters had 3 bedrooms and 2 bathrooms. I'm telling you this was a massive mansion with several out buildings with even more luxurious quarters for the landscapers and production staff.

There were gardens that towered 10 feet tall and meticulously tailored with fountains, and massive statues from around the world. Tours were given daily and on weekends it was packed to the hilt.

My office was above one of the garages and had a fireplace in it. An office with a fireplace? Sweet! I started my new job and truly liked what I was doing, but at the same time my new relationship with the engineer I was heavily dating was blossoming. To the point where he was contemplating moving his whole family to the State I was in.

I didn't want that to happen as for one thing his children were teenagers and heavily involved in school activities. Besides their mom also lived nearby and moving them away after a fairly new divorce is just not a wise idea.

I was much more mobile since my child was grown and already out on her own. I began thinking of what the best strategy would be and I thought of that President of the consulting firm helping me get back on track by utilizing his networking.

I called him up and explained my situation and stated that I wanted to move closer to be near my boyfriend thinking he would know of some connections.

Within a week the President of this consulting company offered me a job as his Office Manager. See, networking and maintaining business cards is so valuable. Again that's the old version of LinkedIn folks (a manual rolodex-ha).

I didn't expect to get a job offer and was shocked about this happening so fast! Conveniently it would be located in only 1 ½ hours from my boyfriend's home and the salary was good so I took the opportunity.

"Mental Zone!"

Wow, what such luck! Later on you'll see why it was lucky at all! We're slowly creeping back into the

Damn! I'm in my forties, my daughter is out of the house, I've maintained a professional demeanor throughout my experiences (until I blow up) and you would think these unbelievably crazy companies/jobs would end, wouldn't you?

Back to my boyfriend……I chose to move that far away as we wanted to introduce me slowly to his children as his divorce was just happening. It was difficult enough to work through that without having me interrupt their healing process at the time.

I hated to tell my current boss that I was leaving already, but she said she knew when she met my boyfriend and how I looked at him. It was only a matter of time. She was very understanding about it and encouraged me to just go with it. I'll never forget that job.

It's was probably the best I had experienced. I even was invited to a capitol building where I met a famous Senator. This Senator took me on a tour of the building and let me sit in his office.

I won't tell you which Senator as that eventually turned into a controversy years later. Not with me but with another person. Hell, he wasn't interested in me…pft.

Eventually I flew over to this new State about a week later to learn more of this new position I was going to take on and search for an apartment or house to rent in a nearby town. The President of the company gave me a tour of the office which was absolutely beautiful.

The building was all glass and right off the main highway. It was architecturally modern. Everything inside the office was in rich greens and mauves. The desks were all expensive cherry and nothing but the best in décor.

He introduced me to all the staff and some of the customers there. Some of the customers gave me a perplexed look, but I didn't catch on why yet. Everyone was extremely professional and pleasant. None knew why I was there or what I would be doing so maybe that's why the funny look on their faces.

As I was touring I notice a gal in the "Office Manager's" office. I inquired about it and the President of the company openly stated <u>right in front of her</u> and everyone that she wasn't working out and was being let go.

What?!

She just hung her head down low. Now with a statement like that I should have gotten a clue that this might not be the right choice. What kind of boss would say something like that in front of everyone?

HUH?! You said that in front of her? In front of everyone? Oh-h-h the hairs on the back of my neck are stiffening up again! Argh. WTF?

I later found out she had been there three years and did a fine job, but the President was tired of her and just decided to let her go. When you are a multi-millionaire there is a tendency you get tired of things easily. Or it seems that way when you see all the stuff they buy or constantly change.

But I was determined to end up close to my boyfriend so I brushed it off. I don't recommend doing that folks as you will later find out.

And I am shocked at myself going through all I've been through so far and still taking jobs that just don't feel right? What am I thinking? You know darn well something isn't right here…but I was in love and being near my boyfriend was my main focus right then.

A week before I was to take my moving truck to this new State I unfortunately was driving to my other part-time job in a really bad rain storm. I was behind a semi hauling logs. He was going very slowly so I decided to pass him.

As I did this all of a sudden the semi decided to swerve in my direction. He couldn't see me in his mirror due to kicking up so much water spray. I had no choice but to turn towards the median.

As I did this I was up to 62 miles an hour so my car decided to flip over (3 times). Yah know it is true what they say. Everything seemed to go in slow motion at that point. My Michael Bolton cassette tape slowly floated past my head. I didn't even know I flipped my car over 3 times.

I landed on the hood and slid over 80 feet on the grass to a stop. I was driving a Pontiac Sunbird. Man, that car saved my life.

Thank goodness there was a guy driving behind me who saw the whole thing. He stated the Tommy Boy thing, **"That was awesome!"** A little later I saw feet and legs upside down, then heard "one-two-three" and my car was flipped upright.

Someone got me out of the car and I started to scream uncontrollably. Someone slapped me to get me to calm down and then I sat in the guy's car that was driving behind me until the police showed up. I was stunned folks. I was to catch a flight to visit my boyfriend the very next morning at 6:00 AM and this had to happen?

My car had one payment to go and just bought new tires. Now it's totaled. And let me tell you something. Once you notify your insurance company you cannot take anything off of the car. You can take your personal belongings but they wouldn't let me have my new tires.

Thank goodness I was alone and did not take my doggy as he would not have survived. However, I had to pick up my Chihuahua from my home base and take him to the vet for boarding right after the accident so I had my current boss drive me there. The vet took one look at me and made me lie down on one of their tables to examine me. Euthanize me now!

He urged me to go to the hospital, but I didn't want to. I felt fine. Thank goodness I was wearing my seat belt as I would most definitely been thrown out of my car.

I got back to the hotel I was temporarily staying in and took a shower. While I was showering I started to bawl uncontrollably again as it all sunk in what just happened. The car was completely gone. But an angel was on my side as it truly was a miracle that I survived such a horrific auto accident.

The next morning I got up to get ready for the airport and I could hardly move folks. I limped to the bathroom and looked in the mirror to see one black eye.

I had to catch that flight so I trudged along and somehow was able to get dressed and get to the airport. My boss was so nice to drive me there. Well I had to forget that part for now and my insurance coverage paid for a temporary car rental which was comforting.

A week later I found a house to rent, packed my things in a little moving truck and moved to this new State.

Chapter XI

This particular company supplied newly laid off Executives private offices, a private secretary, receptionist and job search services.

They would contact major companies and for anywhere from $10,000 to $20,000 a person or group of people and would offer office space and services for 6-12 weeks per person.

This was mainly used for executives who were laid off or let go by companies.

It was a very lucrative business concept and it took much of the burden away from the company doing the layoff or termination. Ironically, one of the VP's from a previous company I worked with ended up there.

I began my role as the previous Office Manager was moving out. Needless to say it was a very uncomfortable first day. As she left, she stated, "Good Luck." She had an uncanny look of relief on her face as she left. Oh Geez, another sign….

I knew I was in a very unstable environment based on the whim of another great leader. Ugh….I'm so very tired of these types of situations. I'd better get the ammo out soon and start polishing my bullets.

I began to learn of what each staff member did. We had three marketing sales managers, three receptionists and 2 secretaries.

The facility was always full which had 13 offices so two secretaries were responsible for 6 or more executives doing all their resumes, recruitment letters and handling their incoming calls.

The beauty of this business is if you get laid off and use one of these offices, no new job prospect had a clue you were laid off as you had a secretary and a physical office. The staff were highly professional and poised.

Once in a while I would hear periodic outbursts from the President's office and most times it was with a marketing sales manager. I tuned it out as best I could since it was getting more and more often. How dumb as clients would hear this too.

There was also an eerie atmosphere in the office. Everyone working there seemed to be acting just like those ladies in the movie "The Stepford Wives."

They were cold, distant and methodical which is what the movie was based on. A robotic type of wife, who followed every command with no emotion. "Perfect." And so were these secretaries.

All the staff were extremely cautious and somewhat nervous with their workloads. Not a lot of chit-chat or laughing. I like to converse especially on breaks to relieve work stress and that wasn't going to happen at this place.

So I stuck to the grind with my duties which were not much at all. Most days I'd be done by noon and didn't know what else to do the rest of the day. But somehow I found other things to occupy my time.

One day the President wanted to change the customer service room so potential touring customers could watch what we do and see our software programs in action.

He asked me to draw a schematic of how to rearrange the customer service and data entry room which was one of the largest areas in that office.

This room currently had three open cubicles but the data entry side was backed into the wall so a customer would not be able to walk around and view how we merged letters into job opening sourcing.

It also seemed somewhat crowded with the filing cabinets in the middle of the room and had a lot of small areas to maneuver in.

My boyfriend and I came up with doing the cubicles in a horseshoe and strategically placing nice floral arrangements or plants in open areas making more room for customers to walk around and view.

The President loved it and said "Go for it." We started working on it that next weekend. As we were rearranging my boyfriend and one of the clients came up with even a better arrangement.

This new idea would be moving all the work stations against one wall and making a complete open area with exotic plants, small love seats, a work table and nice floor lamps. Looking like a much more professional reception area. It opened up that room beautifully.

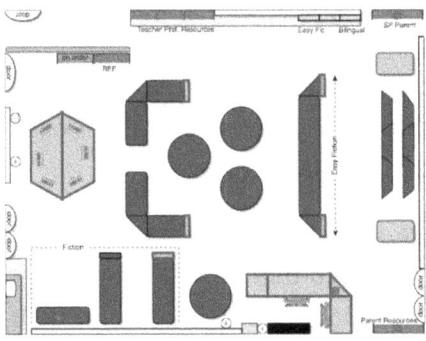

The following Monday the President came into the office...looked around and said that the processing room looked great in front of everyone.

He then calmly asked me to come into his office. Oh boy! I thought he was going to present me with something or personally thank me for all my efforts! **Yah Think?!!**

He calmly proceeded to state......**if I ever change an original approved plan without him authorizing again, that I would be fired immediately!**

What a nice boss!

I then asked him if he wanted me to change it back to the original horseshoe drawing and he said no that he liked it this way better, just after he humiliated me. Naturally I walked out of there feeling very accomplished (sarcasm).

Later that day the President came into my office and told me to take my boyfriend out to dinner and charge it to him for working on the customer service area. What is with this guy?! Positive and negative all day long.

So the next upcoming weekend we went to a restaurant the President referred us to and ordered a nice lamb chop dinner costing about $150.00 when all was said and done.

I came in the following Monday to thank the President for picking up the tab on our dinner and he said "What tab?" I don't know what you're talking about. Is this guy a psycho? I just walked out and didn't say anything.

The dinner was put on his charge account and I never heard any backlash from it. I should have ordered a bottle of champagne - darn it!

As the weeks went on I came into the main office and noticed one of the receptionist's was crying. I pulled her in my office and asked what was going on and she said that she didn't know about a new client arriving in one of the offices and two calls came in for him.

The President was there and listened to her response and screamed at her so loud that she ran to the bathroom to vomit. The President has no professionalism as he does these outbursts right in front of his clients all the time. They don't say anything for fear their services would be cut off.

The receptionist was at least smart enough to take messages acting as if he was there. But it wasn't good enough for the President. This gal was extremely professional in dress and demeanor. Very talented on the computer, she was around 60 years old and always smiled no matter what.

For not knowing this client was there I felt she handled the calls very well. That same week one of the other secretaries was typing a resume, took it back to the client for proofing. Then brought it to me to proof it and yet again another office person proofed it.

All four of us gave the go ahead to run 500 copies and get them out to hiring managers. This was done perfectly and expeditiously.

But...the following week this same client said we had his home address wrong. You know how you feel when walls come crashing down and you have trouble breathing? This is it! This poor gal's eye's bulged out in despair.

We all proofed it including the client, how could this have happened?! I'll tell you how it happened, the client failed to tell us he recently moved. But it ultimately was our fault because we're not mind readers…how unfortunate that we didn't have that gift!

Well naturally this got back to the President and (get ready for it)…**BAM!** He comes in that office, harshly swings the door open until it slams against the wall, runs to my office and demands I meet him in the back where this gal is working. O-o-o-o, I'm so scared O-o-o-o. Not really!

He was so loud that some of the clients came out to see what all the commotion was In front of everyone. He proceeded to ream the life out of this gal. She was 62 and just started to bawl uncontrollably. She ran to the bathroom where I followed her.

We talked at quite length and I advised her to update her resume and start contacting agencies to find her work explaining she can't continue working under these conditions.

She stated she didn't think anyone would hire her at her age and I told her "hogwash," as she had been there five years and never missed a day. She had many years left and a lot of company's prefer a mature person with tons of skills.

I let her know I would give her a fabulous reference. Funny after all this abuse she still wanted to stay there. There's that co-dependent thing again. But moreover, I think it's because of being used to the same work or place.

She was terrified and proofed her work with a fine tooth comb. So afraid of missing a period or comma. The pain and suffering continued until one day he ultimately fired her.

I asked her to meet me after work at a local establishment to talk about this. I also told her I could look at her resume. I hugged her and kept in touch just to be sure she would be okay. On the bright side shortly after she did find another secretarial job at a 1-gal office.

A little less pay but boy was she ever happy to be out of that situation! And she was totally in charge of it all. It's uncanny how none of the office personnel felt they would be able to get a job elsewhere. He must have instilled some sort of brainwashing telling them this.

Another office gal and myself were doing all the typing since they hadn't hired a replacement for the 62 year old gal he recently fired. The work was exhausting.

While typing a very important contract that would net the company around $50,000. I gave it to the other gal to finish as I had to check on the client's needs. Besides she was doing very well with contracts.

She worked on it for about two hours and forgot to give it to me to proof. Instead she delivered it directly to the Vice President of Sales.

Something was odd a few hours later as his door was shut most of the day with the President in attendance. We could hear some yelling going on but couldn't make out anything.

I saw the President leave and as he did, stared at me with leering eyes. By the end of the day the VP of Sales called me into his office, didn't shut the door and proceeded to loudly state how unskilled I was and how he expected more with my credentials. He asked how I could turn in something with so many errors on it.

At the time I didn't know what he was talking about, so he showed me and said, "Didn't you type this?" I told him no that it was the other office gal. I told him I had never seen it.

Now mind you I've never turned anything in before that was inappropriate so wouldn't you think that maybe someone else did it? Not him. Now how was he going to back out of this one?

He said, "Oh" and scrambled to still condemn me for it. It didn't matter but I was intrigued with his scrambling. By the way staff and clients were still in the building.

I kept apologizing and took responsibility because I oversaw the projects. I told him I would have it corrected immediately and resent to him for approval.

For crying out loud, it hadn't gone to the company yet, it was still an internal situation.

He then stated that I was on thin ice with the President and that I probably should start looking for another job.

Oh-h-h…..okay, now I get it. Trying to find a reason no matter what to get rid of me like the other person before me. He's tired of me already? I'm no longer the flavor of the year.

Finally he finished blabbering and I walked out of his office. Now I had only been there 8 months, but I wasn't the type to take any crap and all knew it. Am I getting tougher folks? You bet I am!

He later came into my office and said it wasn't him doing the talking but he was expressing what the President asked him to. He offered to look at my resume and give me advice.

I just sat there and said, "Bill, you are 50 years old and how can you work for someone like this?" He would tell me it's because he gets paid very well. Money talks I guess but not for me.

NO THANKS! I've been doing resume's all my life and didn't need his help. Where are the independent people?! All I keep seeing are "followers" and people who succumb to the whims of poor leaders.

I wasn't really happy to arrive into work that following Monday. Well the President was in rare form that day since he couldn't go home over the weekend (he lived in a Southern State). It's going to be a MONDAY folks!

That morning I brought his mail in and I noticed one of the female Marketing Managers standing in front of his desk, motionless looking straight at him-no conversation. Almost at military attention.

He was shuffling through his papers and didn't even look up at her. It was eerie because he was working on his desk as if she wasn't in the room at all.

I said hi to her. She literally didn't turn her head to notice me when I walked in. I knew something very strange was up.

I laid his mail on his desk and he didn't look at me either but as I s-l-o-w-l-y started to walk out he immediately directed me to stand next to her and not move for 10 minutes.

Oh what hell is this? Oh boy…..well I had an itch on my nose so I scratched it. **Holy Cow!** The world just ended right then and there!

He saw me scratch and said that itch just cost me another 5 minutes of standing motionless staring at this God forsaken man, if you even call him that. Geez! Were thick in the "Mental Zone!"

By now my boyfriend was my fiancé and I thank you for the nice congrats. We discussed this whole mental situation at work. We both thought it was best for me to quit so it was decided to get out of Dodge and quick.

I told a couple of girls I trusted so they would be prepared. They were devastated because they knew even more work would be added to their already heavy loads and they felt I was some type of support or protection for them.

I advised them to get out too. Most of his staff doesn't stay long anyway. There were so many more opportunities in that area and all they had to do was to go out there and grab it. But again that co-dependency just keeps us centered where we are.

This guy always has a box of exquisite chocolates and Cuban cigars on the right side of his desk. So that evening, I placed my resignation smack dab in the middle of his desk with two half eaten chocolates on top of the letter.

I thoroughly enjoyed the condiments sitting in his chair with my feet on his desk. I know that's a little extravagant but I just wanted to do it once. I stopped by the payroll desk and retrieved my paycheck and left for good.

I felt **rejuvenated** and **elated** that I didn't have to go back into that institutional nuthouse the next day! But I felt so sorry for the gals and clients I left behind. Not for long as I was OUTTA THERE! I can only hope they found jobs elsewhere so they could see a better side to careers.

This guy had that Sales Manager gal call my home to tell me to return a pen and pencil set? For one thing I never took anything with me when I left. Absolutely nada. Not even a candy dish I bought. I didn't want any memories of that place-period!

Would you believe he made her call me for four months straight after that? I finally changed my cell number as it was truly a sad situation. She said he was making her do it.

I think it was a cheap pen and pencil set that had a matching clock for a desk. I told her that I last saw it in the customer service office on filing cabinet. Later she called and told me she found it. Now this gal made $65,000 plus commission a year. Again I guess they'll do anything for a good salary.

Chapter XII

My fiancé and I were both 44 at the time and were going to get married within a year so we decided to have me move in with him where he had a nice piece of farm property.

I am someone who has to feel independent so I immediately starting my job search in his area. Luckily he lived only twenty minutes from a large college town which had a University Hospital there.

I took on a temporary assignment for a couple of months at this hospital. I worked in heart failure so when I picked up the phone I would answer it, "Heart Failure, Kate Speaking." I really liked saying that and the job was okay but unfulfilling.

I would stay in touch with their human resources for other opportunities, but nothing ever panned out. I kept getting responses that they didn't have any positions authorized for fulltime, only for a temporary slots.

So I trudged on looking for my next new adventure. By now it was around 1995. I was fortunate to find a Human Resources Management position only minutes from our home. I took a reduction in pay, but it was only a 7 minute drive. They paid me $28,000 which is great for this particular rural area back then.

Now this was an awesome job.

I was there two years. The Plant Manager was a female and she was one who would pitch in if there was a need. Truly hands-on. She taught all of us that when we come to her with a problem we had better have two solutions to offer before we come to her.

She was very community involved as we were business-to-business hosts which means we had other businesses periodically meet in our building to go over economic development and then tour.

Within our own plant she loved to have Monday manager breakfast meetings. So on Mondays all the managers would meet at a local establishment to go over the week's production and other topics along with eggs and bacon! My kind of meeting!

She and I became good friends as well as colleagues. She was on home shopping all the time and she saw what was to be my wedding ring. If you know what a "First Promise" ring is, then imagine the diamond on this as small.

Yup, I was marrying a practical guy! Love isn't about the ring, it's about his life insurance policy. I'm just kidding folks! She was polite about it, but kept showing me the cubic zirconia rings she bought on the home shopping show. I loved one of them and she ordered it for me. (There's a relation to this).

One day I was walking up to the building and I had the most awful chest pain. I had trouble breathing and just couldn't get a grip on things. As I got into the building and started to walk toward my office, one of the maintenance guys was also a paramedic.

They said I looked like crap so he took my blood pressure. 175 over 110. Yup, I wasn't doing too well. So they called an ambulance. I remember getting into the ambulance and my boss yells out "Were is your ring?" WHAT? I'm dying and all she was concerned with was where my ring was? You gotta love her.

The doc couldn't figure out the problem and I got better. Must have been a chemical imbalance or something. Later we would discover a blood pressure problem which was resolved.

Things were going very, very well but gosh darn if a headhunter didn't call me to tell me of a really exciting Regional Human Resources Management opportunity. It paid $42,000 which was about a 40% increase in salary.

It had a company car as this position would travel in between 3 sites at over a 240 mile radius in three States. And the benefits were great!

My conscience weighed heavily especially because of my rapport with my current boss and the close distance from home. This would mean traveling away from my husband 3 days a week too and we just got married.

But I didn't want to pass up such a good opportunity so after discussing with my husband I decided to interview for the position. I really didn't think I interviewed well, but one week later they called and said I got the job. The heck you say!

Now I had the displeasure of notifying my current Plant Manager who also became a very close personal friend. That was very hard for me to do. She was at my wedding and I would go to her home for picnics. She tried to counter offer but it couldn't compare and I wanted to try the idea of traveling.

She was very angry and eventually that also ended our professional and personal relationship.

Chapter XIII

So I moved on and started another new adventure.

This was a plastic injection mold manufacturer. Had three plants in different Midwest States. Due to the distance between them all I was able to spend 1.5 days in each plant, but was mostly on the road constantly. It was okay except for the fact that I didn't see my husband as often as I wanted to.

About 8 months into the job my husband told me his company was transferring him to a Northern Midwest State. I thought this would be okay as one of the plants was in near there and I could make that my base. This would mean a bit more traveling time to the others but my company was okay with it.

Well gosh darn, another 6 months went by and this company decided to shut down this plant location. So now I lived the farthest away from the other two facilities. I mean the closest was a 5 hour drive.

They kept two of the plants but it was not economical and eventually we all figured out that it would be better to hire someone locally for each site. Awwww Geez, now I had to find yet another job! So repetitive!

So I trudged on once again applying for human resources positions within an hour of my home location. I had a lot of interviews but nothing ever became final.

Finally I interviewed with a very large 24/7 manufacturer in the Midwest. I started there at $42,000.

This plant never had an HR Manager there before so with the guidance of the corporate offices in a far West state, I started up a new human resources department.

I handled new policies, job description development, employee disciplines, safety, benefits, awards programs and EEO compliance.

When I was first hired, the Plant Manager gave me about 17 goals to complete. I finished all but one within six months of employment. When I brought all the completed work to him with his list he was dumbfounded to say the least.

He was so impressed that I received a 3% raise mid-year. Everything went smoothly, we all got along and the plant was very productive.

A little over two years went by and my husband notified me that he was again transferring back to a previous facility. I was devastated!

I loved my supervisor, everyone at this facility and especially my new home that I just got acclimated to. I was just getting my routine down and the benefits were magnificent. We tried the commuting thing but it was 5 ½ hours away and became increasingly difficult.

It would be too costly for us to pay two house payments, utilities and gas traveling. Plus I had to take care of the yard, repairs and bills from the main home and handle my job on top of it.

Gosh darn, once again I had to give notice to another company. Once I did that my supervisor changed his demeanor towards me completely. Like night and day.

He was rude, wouldn't talk to me and stayed away. I often thought this was his way of dealing with the emotion of my leaving as we really got along well professionally.

My husband and I also had a nice sized boat so when we were also getting that ready for winter storage when he would drive back up. On the last night before we locked up the boat we went to a friend's wedding being held at the marina restaurant.

Naturally we had too much to drink at this wedding and we walked back to our boat to rest a bit so I jumped inside, caught my foot on the boat ladder and fell backwards. Now the ladder is permanently affixed to the back of the boat and wasn't going anywhere. So-o-o CRACK! Broke my ankle. What a nice feeling that was!

Well my husband was not in a good position to drive me anywhere so we just laid onto our boat bed to rest while I hung my foot out. Around 3:00 am the next morning he brought a dock cart to the boat, I hobbled to it and sat inside.

He wheeled me to the car and we drove to the emergency room. That doctor was so MAD at me for waiting before coming in as the foot starts to heal immediately. Not one of our brighter decisions but we were not in a mode to be driving so I think we made the right choice.

The doctor was able to temporarily set it and told me to see a foot specialist the next day. I did and that doctor told me it was one of the cleanest breaks he's seen and it should heal up rather fast.

In a foot cast and crutches, I was going back to work to finish out my one month resignation notice and my boss noticed my cast on my leg. After that he must have felt compassion as he warmed up to me nicely.

I stayed in touch with him after I left and he later emailed me to tell me he replaced me with a gal that was an ex-cop, but also had some human resources skills.

About 6 months later I heard from my old supervisor again who sent me a card and all that was written on it was "Never hire an ex-cop for a human resources manager." Say no more, that's all I needed to know what he meant. Poor guy….

That was a short chapter folks!

Chapter XIV

Well with another transfer we placed our dream home up for sale and my husband rented a house at his new location until I could get up there. Our plans were to buy a home so that's what I did most of my weekends there…look for a home in a cast on crutches! Man, that was cumbersome especially homes with stairs.

Shortly after I was fortunate enough to gain an interview with a well-known company in the area. I met with the current Human Resources Administrator who was leaving to take a job at a County Office.

The description was everything I've done, payrolls, benefits negotiation, administration, counseling supervisors, hiring, terminations, workers compensation claims and so on.

I did very well at the initial interview phase and soon I was called back for a second interview and met the CFO.

He was different, but all the qualities of a person who watches the books. After completing that interview I was brought into a conference room where the President and Vice President were.

They were a great bunch and I loved them immediately. Well I got the job starting at $45,000. The President, Vice President and CFO all worked out of this facility and they were all brothers.

They had six plants throughout this Midwest state. For laborers, this job was a dirty one. The floor workers sorted through product that was very filthy such as stinky milk jugs, soiled or wet smelly cardboard, papers and cans.

These folks would work on a conveyor line pulling off any product that wasn't recyclable. Then it moved into a machine that automatically sorted it by paper, can or plastic. Very neat operation.

I needed to travel every other week to 5 of the six locations and with having to do weekly payrolls and new hire/termination paperwork, counsel managers and staff (whew) this was difficult to schedule.

At these sights I would make myself visible to all employees and handle all of their questions. I would set time aside to counsel the plant managers and work on workers compensation claims. But all in all I was able to get my niche' going and flowing.

I even had a little time to work on the annual Christmas party which was fantastic. The Christmas party budget was $23,000 which is a lot.

This company spared no expense for the staff. We would have it at an exclusive hotel, each employee was able to have a suite for only $20.00 each, they received all the free beer they wanted and had 4 free mix drink tickets.

The meals were buffet style with 2 meats and numerous condiments. We also purchased about $4,000 in prizes for staff. Had a DJ and we retained business volunteers to run a casino at the party.

Their winnings enabled them to purchase the prizes. It was so much fun for about 200 people and 20 volunteers.

It was great but no time to relax. I would be so keyed up all week that I couldn't calm down during the weekends. I had no help so

I was the only one handling all related paperwork, representing lawsuits and handling disciplines (in person).

Also during this time I joined the local Chamber, HR Association, and SHRM and monthly met with a group of professional gals just to talk. I was starting to get noticed professionally.

In my third year with this company I tried to convince the bosses to hire a human resources assistant for me. But to no avail and I became increasingly despondent because I could NEVER take more than a day off for vacations.

I would always worry about the new work and finishing the old from the previous week. So I struggled with that for another year. Finally in my 4th year I begged and pleaded my case to acquire an assistant. Again, no change. There was no life/work balance.

So ONCE AGAIN…..I decided it was time to seek out a different career. I was fortunate enough to have an interview with an all-encompassing retirement community and nursing home.

They offered me the job starting out at $54,000. It was a good increase in salary and the benefits were very nice. Only a 23 minute drive from my home.

Not only did you get two weeks' vacation and 9 holidays, but you also received an additional 52 hours personal time off days or 6 1/2 extra days that you can use or roll over each year. It was also a Director title and darn it, I earned it so I couldn't refuse it.

When I resigned I attended my last HR group meeting and this group presented me with a beautiful plaque for my contributions. They also told me if I hadn't left I was being nominated for Chairperson. I was honored by that!

But with this new job I realized I finally found my true passion- HEALTHCARE! This was a huge facility with 110 skilled nursing, 60 dementia, 80 assisted living and 90 independent residents.

A massive 2-story horseshoe style building with about 20 cottages surrounding it on 28 acres. It also had a basement level where the beauty parlor, convenient store, exercise, game and craft rooms were.

Upper level had a church that could hold 200 people, a café/gift shop, another beauty parlor and activity rooms.

It was a very well kept building with grandfather clocks, grand pianos, large palm and exotic plants, 300-gallon fish tanks and an enormous and gorgeous dining room buffet style with white linens and fresh flowers.

We had several Chefs. The kitchen alone had 40 staff and the rest added up to a total of 230 staff members. Yes, I handled all 230 plus worked closely with other managers by myself. No assistant. But it was different here. I didn't have to travel, I was able to focus on HR only and didn't do payrolls so it was manageable.

This was a well-run ship by a very seasoned and great Administrator. To this day I wish I had never left that position. But something happened about 3 years later of doing this daily where everything just caught up with me and I lost it.

It was a massive feeling of being overwhelmed probably due to having to hire about 300 people consistently. Normally I can handle anything, but this time I just totally lost it. I remember walking down a hallway and just bursting out in tears. I ran to the ladies room and just bawled.

I wish now that I had just requested a week off to rest and get myself back to where I needed to be. I just needed to get away a bit. But after being there over 3 years and truly loving every minute of it my husband stated he had received another transfer to another State but on the farthest end of it so he was over four hours away. I couldn't possibly keep this job.

Chapter XV

Oh-h-h-h-h, the pain of having to find another job, home and move again. This was getting exhausting but mostly now becoming more emotional as I really liked it there.

So by now it's the year 2008. We settled into a nice townhome and I immediately started to job search. Due to this city and suburbs being large in size and having an abundance of manufacturing or professional sectors it wasn't long before I had quite a few interviews lined up.

Within 2 weeks I had several offers from various Human Resources Management positions in the same week. One on an older part of the city, kind of crime ridden actually for another recycler that knew my previous boss; one for a home health company and the other for a corporate consulting firm in a nice suburb.

Never have I had three offers within the same week! Boy was my head ever swollen over that.

All were extremely competitive with their overall compensation and benefit package, but I ended up accepting the corporate human resources management one in the nicer and closer suburb.

I felt this was the best challenge for me since it had global exposure which intrigued me. This was a consulting firm that had 80 employees and 120 contract employees in about 23 States so this would also give me exposure to multi-state regulations and law.

Two weeks before I started one of the Vice Presidents gave me a tour of the new building they were moving into. This was a gorgeous three story building with a beautiful atrium and balcony to all the offices.

We basically took up half of the top floor. In back of the building there was a huge deck with tables and a pond with a spectacular fountain in it.

It was right next to the city's main golf course so during lunch you can walk the trails near it and see all the beautiful plants. The staff were all professionals, normally in business casual dress unless special guests would be coming.

The President was a warm person who thrived on enabling his staff to do their best. My office was in the middle section between two engineering consulting offices.

Things were going along nicely for about a year and a half. I developed a "paperless" filing system where you pretty much set up your employee files on the computer and saved them there.

Now besides doing payrolls, hiring, orientations, workers compensation, leave of absences, etc. I also tracked vacation days or illnesses.

As I was tracking absences, I periodically would submit a monthly report to the department managers showing where their people were at in attendance. We had a policy in place and some were starting to exceed the limits and nearing warnings.

Two specifically in the accounting department. I would bring their attendance record to their manager and he would argue with me over it as he continually approved them and did not want them counted. However, other managers were applying the policy with due diligence to their staff. I did my best to explain that this was inconsistent with the policy to no avail.

Now, I'm not a hard-nosed stick to the policy kind of person, once in a while a pre-excused or emergency situation is fine, but not 19 absences within 3 months.

And as you know other staff notice this and began complaining that this was unfair. When their department managers wanted to write someone up I referred to these two accounting personnel and said we really couldn't do it and remain consistent. It was turning into a morale issue. It was my responsibility to uphold our policies.

I have to take a moment to give you an idea of what this one particular manager was like. This was a pretty crude person for such a professional office and exposed that to all many times. The "F" bomb word was second language for this manager.

This manager had a history of roughness and the way the conversations went made you uncomfortable or nervous as you would be tested for bravery speaking with them. Almost like a show off but in a scary way.

I remember telling their boss six months into the job that I felt this person was dangerous. I couldn't pin a finger on what, but my sense kept telling me to keep a distance with this manager. This gut feeling would later be reaffirmed in my book.

This manager always complained of not having enough time off and I would just absorb the complaint. This was one who was consistently late sometimes up to a couple hours a day. One month this manager took off 4 work days to travel out of State to see relatives.

About 3 months after that trip this person wanted to see how many days they had left and I showed only 2 days left. I told this person that they took four days of vacation to go out of town. This manager said they were here working and can prove it.

The manager went back on their computer to show me emails sent on those days. I said that didn't prove anything, this person had email capability anywhere they went if they took their laptop. This made the manager mad who then said, "So you don't believe me?" I said it's not that at all.

I then pulled their file up on the computer and found the vacation request form they filled out which was also signed by their supervisor and I ran a copy of it. This manager was getting pretty unhappy by now and it showed in their demeanor towards me.

The manager now claimed they never took those days and tore up the request. So I went into the payroll for that week and AGAIN showed them I entered the vacation days as PTO on their paycheck and that must have been it, as nothing was said after that.

I then went to that manager's boss to inquire on those dates off and he confirmed the dates of absence. Want more confirmation?! Now here is where it gets bad ladies and gentlemen.

When I was reconfirming with this manager the dates they were gone, I would show this manager my notes regarding dates of absences. Only if I am aware as sometimes the department managers just say so and so is off today. I do this for memory and situations such as this one.

It's nothing private or confidential. It just helps me track time off. No big deal really. I even do that now. I not if they called in sick or if the car broke down or if the weather caused it, etc. Nothing to get alarmed over for heaven's sake.

This manager asked to see these notes next to their days off. Again these were just notes saying "off ill" or "vacation" or "emergency." Holy crap! This manager then became very upset. Here's what ticked them off, I also showed tardies as "in late."

I note everything folks and I have the right to! I was starting to get more frustrated with this person as I knew what they were doing. The manager finally stormed out of my office. Sheesh that was a whole hour of explaining.

Well they weren't gone long (darn it) and the manager later came back in and said I was right but was upset that they now didn't have enough time off for an upcoming family reunion.

I finally blurted out, "Do you want me to just give you some days back, and is that it?" I advised they talk with their supervisor and see if something could be arranged. There's always options, just talk it over with him.

As long as it was approved, I really couldn't do anything about it. Well, this manager didn't want to do that as they knew their boss wouldn't authorize it as he knows what this manager's attendance has been.

After that happened this manager's whole demeanor towards me changed as if this was my fault. This manager purposely stayed away from me, when I walked past them in the hallway, this manager started to choke and gag.

The comment was made that it was my perfume. Oh please! Grow up! I wasn't even wearing any perfume. Now I know a lot about common sense and it was prevalent among the other staff seeing all this going on.

They just stared. Who could say anything when you have immaturity like that? One of the supervisor's rolled their eyes over it in disgust.

The following few weeks I noticed a bunch of girls going into this manager's office a lot and closing the door. I didn't think anything of it. I know they were rumoring. Pettiness begets Pettiness. And let me tell you, when you have an abundance of close staff in a manager's office you have a RUMOR MILL.

I don't care what anyone says it's happened at every single darn job I've held! Even with men! Well one of the gals that would frequent this manager's office gave her resignation to another manager.

I was in a meeting with the higher ups and didn't hear about it until the manager walked in the meeting to tell us which was around 5:00 pm.

The higher personnel looked at me and looked at the other VP who was also in the meeting, slammed his fist on the table and asked me, "What is your job here? What good are you? Didn't you see this coming?

NOT AGAIN!
NOT AGAIN!
NOT AGAIN!
NOT AGAIN!
NOT AGAIN!

I explained that I didn't see this coming at all and I just found out with the rest of them. Then he said he was very disappointed with both of us and walked out. The other VP just shrugged his shoulders and left stating that the President didn't understand and is making assumptions.

Was that to appease me or make me feel better? It didn't! At least I wasn't solely blamed. How could I know? There wasn't a clue this employee was leaving.

By then it was 6:00 pm and the gal had left for the day. The very next morning I immediately went to her and asked her why she was leaving and she said she found a better job. I then said is there anything we can negotiate on to keep her here? She said no.

I joked that I wasn't going to let her go and she just stared at me. I could feel something really wrong was going on but I just couldn't figure out what it was.

Now I've always had a great rapport with this gal, we even used to eat lunch together and talk about our families. All of a sudden she was standoffish and rude with me? Almost like a hatred towards me. I got along with all the staff so this was getting stranger by the day.

Well I would soon discover why all of this was happening and it will make sense at the end of this. About a month later the VP asked me to come into his office to review the resignation letter.

The letter had all kinds of statements against me personally and professionally. Oh what kind of hell is this now? What is going on around here?!!

This gal said she was leaving because of me, that I couldn't keep anything confidential, that I violated HIPAA and on and on. I was shocked! The letter was typed almost as if an attorney wrote it.

I told him that none of this was true. By the way HIPAA was spelled wrong in the letter (this will be a huge clue later on in this book).

You see, this gal had seizures which she told me about. I never inquired on what from or anything, but she was telling me she might need intermittent FMLA and I said that was fine. I did ask her if we needed to be aware of anything if she has a seizure at work and she said to just leave her alone and let the seizure pass.

I told her I must notify her direct supervisor and stated it would remain confidential. She was okay with that. I received her medical condition with the FMLA paperwork and filed it.

I felt it was proper to explain the situation with her direct supervisor who is the VP of Administration in the event it occurs at work so someone knew and also prep them that she might be taking a few days off here and there with intermittent leave.

I never gave out any medical condition or medication or anything. Just to be aware and to not do anything that might cause more harm if she had a seizure. I advised the manager and VP to keep this highly confidential.

Well that didn't work as her supervisor told this manager that was pissed at me. How did I find out? Because the mad manager walked into my office one day and said, "Oh by the way, you should never perform CPR on anyone who has seizures."

I asked them what they were talking about and this manager said I know about so and so because her manager told me.

Oh gosh….I hung my head low! This damn manager told the VP who became concerned that we leaked it out and came into my office and asked me to call our corporate attorney. Now wouldn't you ask me first what happened?

The attorney explained that I had done nothing wrong and did all the right things. I hadn't violated any HIPAA law and that I was legally obligated to notify this gal's boss in the event something does happen so people don't rush to her and do the wrong thing. Life goes on.

I started to feel awful. The fact that my integrity was being compromised didn't sit well with me. Also the gal's direct supervisor fessed up to being the leak. It's my responsibility to do what is best for the protection of others.

If another manager chooses to breach a confidentiality then it's on their head. Not mine. They knew it should be kept secure. That's not my responsibility and that should be addressed separately. Well eventually that gal left and things were about the same in the office.

The manager I ticked off before kept avoiding me and more gals would meet in their office under a closed door. I just stuck my nose to the grind. I mean what can you do? Nothing...this person had such a hold on people. They felt powerful around this manager.

One of the VP's who is a female lived in another State and while on a mini vacation had an extremely serious illness. I immediately place her on FMLA and kept in contact with her as she was obviously an emotional wreck.

I received her physician documents later and just filed them accordingly. I told her boss who is the President that should would be out for at least 3 weeks with a serious health condition.

He asked me what it was and I told him I couldn't reveal it as it was a private female situation and it wouldn't affect him, he understood. Gee do you think I just reinforced my integrity? Same ole stuff.

I know this seems like I'm getting off track but it'll all come into play soon.

A couple of months later the higher ups wanted to do an employee survey on the company overall. We used Survey Monkey. Well the results came back and he called in all the VP's and me to go over them. 35% of the responses were such as:

I don't trust Human Resources

She can't maintain confidentiality

She violates HIPAA (by the way this also was spelled wrong- AGAIN) in the survey no doubt (things starting to piece together here? Yah think?) Come on…you know you are starting to figure this one out!

All the higher ups just looked at me perplexed and I felt like vomiting. Now I was surprised that one of the VP's defended me and said it was probably someone who recently quit. What a great guy he was!

Also the female VP from another state that I processed an FMLA for also stated that I never revealed her situation with anyone so she couldn't understand these statements.

I was dumbfounded as we had to act on these comments since it was an employee survey. **_Things were just not adding up_**. By now I was starting to think about looking for another job as this was becoming an unhealthy situation for me. When you can't control things you just back down.

About another six weeks went by and another gal started going into this same ticked off manager's office with the door shut. Well it wasn't long before she also gave her resignation notice.

I immediately went over to her and told her how sad it was that she was leaving. She told me she was getting her Bachelor's in Human Resources and would do a much better job than me.

What? She will be an awful HR person! She has no clue. Judgmental, prejudice, reactive and MEAN! Yah, she'll go far in HR. Wait a minute. That IS a majority of HR professionals! NOT!!

I thought, oh no, not another one. What was going on around here? When I did her exit interview she was horrible. Told me to hurry up as she didn't want to be near me. At this point I was no longer suspicious but knew something concrete was happening here. **_Something really bad._**

I used to get along with this gal very well also. What made them turn on me? Nothing had changed. Right up to a month before she quit we were laughing and talking. Am I in a bad dream? Is it something in the water? I would consult with one of the other manager's just to get some support.

This manager I talked to was very nice and felt awful about these things. She told me that there's a "click" here but I never noticed it.

It's like having a great friend and the next day they're all of a sudden your enemy. I am probably the most approachable and friendly professional around. There was something very odd going on here! I felt like a sitting duck. Bang-Bang!

My husband was transferring to a more Southerly State and we were doing the commuting thing for a year. One Friday after a week of hell at the office with all this crap I left a little early to pick my husband up at the airport.

As I drove back home my cellphone rings. It's the manager I had confided in for support. She's never called me on my phone so this was strange.

She asked me how I was doing and I just all out BAWLED like I haven't cried in years! In between sobs I stuttered out that I wasn't okay at all. That something was strangely wrong at work. My husband's face was just in awe over this. I don't think he realized how tough this has been on me.

She was genuinely concerned or she wouldn't have called me. She knew something. I told her I didn't know what was going on but it was obvious someone was trying to hurt me or set me up big time.

It's like one of those awful movies you watch where no one believes you but when you see the movie, it's really happening to that person who keeps trying to convince others to believe her.

She was very compassionate and told me she was so sorry for all these things happening and advised me to try to relax and to enjoy my weekend because it was about to change.

I didn't understand what she was saying as it made no sense to me and I was in a break down mode-totally lost by now. I thought maybe she was going to plead my case for me to the President. I just didn't know.

She's an older seasoned gal who had been with the company overall around 15 years and with our ages so close, we got along great. She was aware of my work ethic and management style, so she knew the real story on me.

Well, it was not the greatest weekend. I tried very hard not to think of all the horrible things that happened in the last month, but it had such an impact on me. Mostly because none of it made any sense.

You know how you retrace your thoughts just because you want to make some sense of it? There's a reason I couldn't make anything of it and just kept spinning the information over and over in my head.

My husband, bless his heart was extremely supportive but at a loss as to what to do. He did tell me he would support my decision to just leave as this wasn't worth it. I was thankful he believed me.

I just couldn't fathom what turned all the staff against me? What did I do? What was it? This is where I lost 30 pounds over this ordeal. Even though it's pleasant to lose weight. I wouldn't recommend doing it this way.

Well after an unrestful weekend I went unto work that following Monday. Started my day like I always do. I avoided going into the break room because you have to pass this ticked off manager's office to get there.

It was eerily quiet that Monday. Everyone had their heads down and focused on their work. You could say hi and they would quietly say hi back. Something was in the air that day. The manager that talked to me was in and would smile at me when she walked by but she also seemed a little nervous.

It was late afternoon that the VP of the office asked me to see him. He instructed me to shut his door and to sit down. He was overly nice and offered me some coffee.

I thought that maybe the President wanted him to do my firing and this is how he eased into it. But that wasn't the case here.

Now I've been through a lot of things (oh hell yah!) but this one is another shocker. I mean WOW....wait until you hear this one. (I must be shooting blanks as I'm still here).

He then talked with me about some new information he just received regarding all the things happening to me. Okay, what is this all about? He explained this information and my mouth just dropped.

Evidently a person of interest wanted to make me look totally incompetent for whatever personal reason they had. This VP had evidence and a witness and told me that they were going to bring this person of interest in to approach them over it and told me to be "prepared" when he does this.

Prepared for what? He really didn't give me any concrete information so I knew nothing really. I was so curious what he knew but I now think back that maybe they didn't give me all the concrete evidence knowing I could use this against them or this person? I'm just not that way.

He then told me he found out that one of the managers was heavily involved with the resignation letters, coaching the two employees on their termination and if he could prove that this manager also tampered with the Survey Monkey results and some other things he was going to fire them that day.

I ALMOST FAINTED! I knew something was wrong, but I would never have imagined something as devious as this. Here's how he found out.

I'm a firm believer of what goes around, comes around. Time and time again I hear of destructive people ending up with more harm to them in their lifetime so I'm confident it all works out eventually. Damn Optimism!

Evidently the nice manager who consoled me and the ticked off manager would smoke together outside during breaks. The ticked off manager assumed that their friendship with this nice manager was strong and told her everything including all the sabotaging they were doing to me. All of it. No detail left out.

This didn't sit well with the other nice manager's conscience and due to hearing of all the stuff happening to me and seeing me suffer she eventually told her boss of the dealings.

The VP said he was going to meet with this manager the next day. The next day he called this manager into his office and shut the door. They were in there together over an hour and not one sound came out of there.

He ended up giving this manager a final written warning on the information he knew they had been involved in for sure. Suddenly the door opened and this manager hastily walked past my office crying profusely.

This manager stopped back and stepped inside my office door to tell me they were leaving for the day and that I knew why. I just sat there and stared back. What should you say to that? It wasn't my place to say anything. I didn't know what transpired.

Wait just a doggone minute. Why would this manager AGAIN make a statement that should make me feel bad for their actions? Oh yeah, that makes total sense. WHATEVER! Nothing will compare to the suffering that manager did to me. Absolutely nothing!

A few minutes later this VP dropped off a two page final written warning regarding what this manager had done and asked me to file it. He then shook my hand and said he was sorry for all that had happened and hoped I could let this go on the wayside and walked out. That was it?!

I found out so much more, but again at this point new information wasn't going to impact the outcome one way or another. Like I told them, this person was trouble. I knew it the moment I got to know this manager.

I seem to remember something the other manager said to me. That this person assisted with their resignation letters. I decided to pull them up just to look at them.

I placed them right next to each other and discovered the core portion of the letters were nearly IDENTICAL! Yet from two different people, a month apart.

And yup, the word HIPAA was misspelled in both letters. At first I didn't know how to respond because I didn't know where he was going with this. I was definitely flabbergasted but curious where this was heading. Oh Geez Louise.

I remember when this manager first started and they would tell me about their last job and how they were set up to fail. H-m-m-m-m, awfully similar circumstances here. When they told the story, it didn't seem real, like out of a movie. Now we know……

It was awful hearing all of it, but also a good thing so I could grasp the level of meanness this and other people are capable of. The nice manager liked me a lot and knew I was doing a great job but I sure was starting to get some doubts about my abilities there.

She just couldn't stand seeing anyone purposely hurt another person. It was immoral and had to put a stop to it. OMG…a HUG LOAD off of my brain, heart and body! I was so thankful that the VP believed her. But again they also had some solid information to conclude some of this stuff.

She hugged me and told me everything would be better from now on. The President also stopped by my office to tell me he found out about it and that I did do everything appropriately and that we should just move on.

I knew that was his way of saying he was sorry. By now, it was also mute. He is a great person and should not have to deal with this stuff, but he should have supported me until all this came to light. But again it was stacked up against me and this horrible person setting me up was so meticulous covering their tracks. So I don't blame him at all. Who would? When he found out...he probably couldn't grasp it all at the time either.

I will repeat this time and time again that too many leaders listen to only one side of a story and react only on that information alone. We must take a step back and thoroughly and I mean thoroughly ensure all the stories have been told, all the facts and documentation has been received before we make any decisions at all. It's all about integrity folks.

I hold no grudges. I could have sued the company and this manager personally for that, but I'm just not that type of person.

Forgive and forget. I can forgive but I'm **never ever** going to forget this. I pray that this manager has indeed changed from this incident, but I doubt it because similar has happened in their life before.

They are just too domineering a personality, on the home front as well as work. They can show deep caring and affection one day and turn on you the very next day.

The following Monday this manager came in and naturally due to the uncomfortable situation just avoided me altogether. I still didn't go into the break room. I just didn't feel like seeing this person anymore either. That took a huge toll on me.

I have such a hard time believing these people actually exist in the workforce. I cannot fathom such horribleness by anyone to be this way. What do they gain from it? Does it make them feel good to hurt another human being so badly? You are toying with their lives. Hitting all the sectors such as emotions, physical stress, causing great doubt of the person you are targeting. This is how SUICIDES happen. Geez Louise!

These managers are parents of children. Leaders of other people. Is this what they teach them as okay to do? If so, we are sorely headed in the wrong direction.

I actually got the feeling that this manager felt justified and that none of this was their fault at all just from the way they told me they knew. God was that office quiet after that. Every time I moved all eyes were on me, but eyes with compassion and sorrow. I know all of them believed this other person and now once they realized the truth, they had "Shame" in their eyes.

It's okay…I understood and slowly we got the office back to where it should be, but by then it was over for me. I couldn't stay. The harm was done. There was no healing because this person still worked there. I felt the punishment wasn't justified. A slap on the hand and that was it? It became constructively unbearable and if you are in human resources you know what that term means. It means, when someone or others make work life impossible.

Chapter XVI

Well because my boss didn't believe me or support me initially during this tragedy I decided I just couldn't work there anymore. Too much had happened over such a long period of time that I felt it was irreversible. So with my husband transferring to another state this was a perfect exit for me.

I needed to get as far away from that place as possible. It was very sad as I truly loved that job and most of the people I worked with. It was an exciting position with all the Global interaction.

BUT NOW It was <u>my turn to give notice</u>. I went into the President's office and told him the reason was due to my husband's relocation. I know, I know it's not the real reason, but what good is it to say anything?

He did ask me what I would recommend for the company since I was leaving and of course I stated, "Believe in your people and support them." "Let manager's manage." I was taken aback when he said, "Point well taken" and he thanked me with a hug.

I knew again that this was his way of saying he very sorry for the whole thing. I still stay in touch with him today. And I really feel he'll take that suggestion into consideration going forward.

On my last day the whole office took up a collection and gave me a very nice gift. They also had cake and ice cream for me. It felt very nice. The scorned manager attended and just stared off into space.

I could tell they couldn't wait for this little ceremony to end so they could leave. I know I impacted them as I still get emails from quite a few still today. I have to take a deep breath for a moment as all of this is catching up to me reminiscing.

Okay I'm rested.

Now onto another great adventure! **Oh Yeah Baby!**

I started slowly moving bits and pieces every time I drove out to my husbands. I also cruised the internet for jobs but there wasn't much in this new area. Also what a difference in pay! Awful.

Houses and taxes were cheaper there and wages were substantially lower. I mean earning $40,000 is considered executive pay. That's horrible for working now. I left this job earning over $78,000.

One night my husband and I were walking into the local department store and I decided to grab a Sunday paper. I never use the Sunday paper, but for some reason I did that day. As I was reviewing the jobs I came across a small 2" x 2" ad for an Executive Director of a Retirement Community.

Now I thought I've worked in retirement communities but not at this level. Could I do it? Did it require licensure? I read the job summary and it showed basically managing staff, building repairs, budgets, vendor relations....heck yah, I can do that for sure! This was more or less similar to an office manager role.

I applied to the email address Sunday around 6:00 pm. At 9:00 pm on that same day I got a call from the Regional Operations Manager wanting to interview me the next day.

This was certainly good because I had intended on returning back to my current home that day to pack up some more stuff. I said sure and told her she certainly didn't waste any time. She laughed.

I went to the in person interview, and this place was absolutely beautiful, just gorgeous. I met my boss at the door and as soon as I saw her I felt a great warmth come over me. We had a terrific interview and I met all the staff and residents.

I left there in a gait walk...so excited (and hopeful). The building was so pristine. The décor was exquisite. They had 2 beauty salons, a library, movie theatre, gorgeous dining rooms, a café, and gardens with a gazebo, all the amenities to retire in.

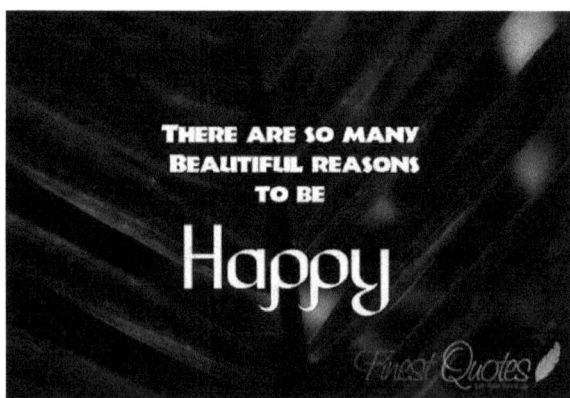

The next phase was to interview with the corporate manager over the phone and that went very well. This corporate manager told my soon to be boss that if she didn't hire me she would. What a nice compliment that was.

Then the final interview was with the key management staff via conference call and that also went great. I got the job offer within a few days of all the interviewing. I accepted and now had to hurry up and get totally moved to this new State.

This wasn't a State I would say I felt good about as it's the same one I lived in when I had that car accident with my daughter in the hospital. But it was a lot farther away in a Southerly direction and was close to mountains with terrific views.

My husband had rented a two-bedroom apartment and it was nice, but only one bathroom. I have to have my own space in that area so a few months later we bought a nice home and moved in. My new career was such a challenge as I was in charge of everything. I was "DA BOSS!" Probably the highest level in a professional role I've ever held.

I managed all the building repairs, landscaping contracts, hiring, terminations, moving in residents, moving out residents, invoicing their monthly rents, maintaining departmental budgets and handling concerns with family members and staff. Only 45 staff and 125 residents. Manageable, but often overwhelming at times.

I put in massive hours, I mean 70-80 a week, but it wasn't something I wouldn't complain about as it was enjoyable rewarding work. Helping elderly with a better quality of life is priceless.

Do you realize most of these people were Presidents or owners of successful companies? We even had a famous college coach and previous senator there. "I found my passion" and that's in assisted living healthcare.

When I arrived I immediately knew that the majority of staff were not dedicated nor had the company's interest at heart. They would saunter when walking or walk past garbage in the hallway and leave it there. No one was energetic nor had a sense of urgency. It was blah or meh.

I had one young gal that's done just about every job there. She's was a Certified Nurse's Aide, former Life Enrichment Manager and then Marketing Director. A woman of many hats. She mastered all incredibly well. She would do anything for you. Many days when a department was short staffed she would help out. Whatever it takes. She was adorable.

I would work with all of the staff trying to get them where they needed to be. Unfortunately, I had to terminate and replace much of the staff as sometimes you just can't change a person. All terminations are not easy and that's an inevitable human resources function.

My management style is terminating with respect as what good does it do to be rude or mean during a termination? It's just not a good fit so end it appropriately.

I literally had to let over 18 staff go and 3 were Directors. Sometimes you need to clean house and replace it with new to get the environment back where it needs to be.

I had a previous Marketing Director that always did things her way and didn't want to follow the Corporate's marketing strategies.

When I first started there she acted as if she was the boss of the facility.

She was extremely overbearing and would talk to you as if you were beneath her. I would listen to her talking to potential residents and most of the conversations were about her and all the nice things she owned. She had this very prominent diamond ring that she continually flaunted at everyone. Or she would talk about her trips to Europe.

I could tell she was totally turning off the potential customer and I noticed she wasn't really listening when the potential customer would talk.

When you have a potential family checking our services and homes out, you treat them as if they were King and Queen. THEY should be the center of attention not us. Well sales were few and far between so I had decided to reign her in and give her a few goals focusing on a new customer approach.

I specifically laid out all the objectives in great detail, then went over it with her to ensure she fully understood. When I do these I reassure that employee of how much I value them and that I'll do everything in my power to get them where they need to be. When I was explaining all this she would doodle on a piece of paper and not look up at me.

So I knew she wasn't really listening or taking this seriously. But I followed through with the timeline asking her progress and she would always come back with reasons why they weren't accomplished.

I finally had to place her on a final plan of improvement with more concrete goals specifically improving sales by a certain time. She was humiliated by this. How dare I put her on a final plan of improvement? The nerve of me! Well this must have set her off more than I thought as she resigned the next day.

The Regional Operations Manager and I interviewed and hired another gal that had a very nice personality. She was dressed very nice, easy to talk to and very confident. She kept telling us of her love for older residents.

My only concern with her was that she had been a previous Administrator and now she was taking on a job as a Marketing Director which the pay difference was quite substantial. Like $60,000 a year less in pay. Who does that?

But she convinced us she would make a difference on the job. She had been looking for a long time and I knew she needed a job. She actually applied for mine when it first came out and I found out she didn't get it and I'm not sure why.

This new marketing director did great for about 2 months and then she would misquote costs or forget some of the pricing which was difficult to explain this to the new tenant. So I typed up a cheat sheet for her to take on her desk and that way she would quote everything correctly.

But she still was misquoting customers. Once they sign that contract with all the numbers on it, that's it. You can't go back and say, "Oh we miscalculated a number so we'll need to increase this." Nope, that signed contract remains for one year.

This gal she would tell me that when she was an administrator she earned over $100,000 a year. About a month later she would tell me the same story but the salary went to $125,000 a year.

After a couple more months the salary was at $150,000 a year and she had an automobile that talked to her. Funny thing is she was totally broke now and married a guy that was not considered financially well off.

In fact she couldn't afford a regular phone so they had a Magic Jack system for a phone at $19.00 a month. Something wasn't right with all the stories, but it wasn't my interest to meddle. Who cares anyway? I had to focus on the now.

She also would disappear a lot. Or go on sales calls much too long. One day she said she was going to "pound the pavement" and gave me a list of all the potential clients she was going to visit that day.

Well we had an outside event that our bus was taking residents to. On the way to the event, they passed the Marketing Director's sister's home and saw the Marketing Director's car there. When they returned three hours later, the Marketing Director's car was still in the same spot.

I remembered she gave me the list of companies and families she was going to see so I decided to do some public relations work myself and started to contact a couple of the clients she was visited to ask if all their questions were addressed during the meeting. None stated that they had seen the Marketing Director that day.

She got back in the next day and I confronted her about it and she said she had gotten suddenly ill and ended up staying at her sisters for the day. DARN! Always an alibi.

I told her she needed to call me when that happens and also notify all the appointments she made to cancel as a courtesy. She said she understood and I documented our conversation. (Remember folks, document everything! Any instruction given so you can say we talked about it). Very, very important.

We had an emergency situation over the summer one year where our power went out for three days due to historically bad storms.

I called all the managers and staff to come in if possible and naturally couldn't get through to the Marketing Director as Magic Jack phone systems are terrible. I called my manager who was going to come over and help out as well.

All the managers came in to help. I was there 36 hours before the Marketing Director finally showed up.

36 STRAIGHT HOURS folks with no sleep. Did I look great? Heck no! Looked like I had been run over by a truck.

This manager was late as she said that her town had power and she assumed we did too. I asked her about my messages and she said her phone doesn't work where she lives. I then asked her if she knew on the news that other towns were without power and she said yes.

I then told her that she must call us to ensure everything was okay and not assume. Wouldn't you at least call in to make sure all was okay?

I knew she was lying as it was all over the local news on TV and radio. In fact, her sister lived 4 miles from our facility and her power was out. I was too tired and ticked at her to argue over it.

My boss and I were sitting at a table figuring out schedules and the Marketing Director looked at me dumbfound and said "What do you want me to do now?" I was so exhausted and just flabbergasted that she didn't have the sense to just look around and ask if anyone needs help. It's just beyond me that anyone can be like this.

I told her to check on the residents since our fire alarms were not working. That per law we had to check all apartments every 15 minutes and indicate this on a compliance form for the State. I was getting more and more frustrated by this. Since my boss and Marketing Manager were there I went home to get a few hours of sleep.

I was shaking so bad when I got home. My husband was so good about it. He kept everything quiet so I could sleep. A few hours of rest made a huge difference.

By the third day without power ours was restored to normal. I bought pizza for all staff that helped out during that time and personally gave each a $10.00 gift card to a local eating establishment. I praised them all week for their efforts as I couldn't have done it without them.

After all that settled about two months later we had another major outside marketing and activity event where we invited the public elderly residents to join. We were taking them to a casino which was two hours away.

We lined up a larger bus due to inviting the public and the Life Enrichment Manager, the Housekeeping Supervisor and Marketing Director were there as chaperones.

Curiously as I got on the bus and checked on the passengers I noticed that the Marketing Director also had her husband, her husband's brother and his wife, her father-in law and her sister all in attendance at our expense.

Now I know if you have all those family members, you are going to be having fun with them and not the residents you are supposed to entertain and chaperone. I didn't say anything as I didn't want to cause a scene or spoil other attendee's fun. I can bring this concern up with her when she got back.

By the end of the day around 6:00 pm they all got back, the Life Enrichment Manager walked up to me and informed me that the Marketing Director was nowhere to be found after they got to the casino.

They saw her during meal times, but that was it. They were hustling to ensure the other 12 residents were having a good time and being watched.

When they all boarded the bus at the end of the event, the Marketing Director said to the Life Enrichment gal that she was a bit tipsy after some drinks and didn't know if she could climb the bus steps (and laughed it off).

When I heard this I was livid! Not only was this gal not watching residents for safety reasons, but she was representing our company on company time. What? How? Damn I'm so frustrated by now. Drinking while taking care of elderly residents? On company paid time? What was she thinking?

I was way to ticked and upset to talk to her then. In my professional career I know it was best to calm down and discuss this appropriately. So I had the other two employees document what they saw and heard and instructed them to give me the facts in the morning.

The next morning the Marketing Director was out doing client and business calls so I called the Regional Operations Manager and asked her to come out to discuss this with me.

Due to the previous lies and continual poor performance (and only being at the company 6 months), then this last serious drinking deal, we decided to terminate her immediately. She put all those residents and staff at risk. That's one Director I unfortunately had to terminate.

Now I needed to replace her. I had some documentation showing that the Life Enrichment gal would be a good fit and would work three times harder. The Regional Ops Manager agreed and we promoted her to Marketing Director.

Her salary went from $12.50/hour to $40,000 a year. Boy was she ever happy. I remember her letting out a surprise noise and ran over to my office to show me her first big paycheck. That was so neat! She was a very proud gal.

We advertised and hired another Life Enrichment Manager who turned out fantastic too!

I had another Director who was a very harsh, direct and didn't handle nursing infractions at all. This Director would talk to the staff by belittling them.

This person would openly call staff "idiots" during our manager's meeting. There started to be discrepancies in certain report audits so I eventually placed this Director on a plan of improvement as well.

At first there was a slight improvement and I always commented to this person how great this improvement was to keep them pumped up. But eventually it went back to being their old ways.

Staff were constantly coming into my office stating they couldn't work for this Director anymore. All falls, injuries or deaths get called to me all hours of the night and one night I came in and saw that this one nurse had been using our guest suite to sleep in and had their dog in it.

I informed this nurse that they can't do that. On another occasion I was walking down the hall and notice a cup of pills sitting on the floor near a resident's apartment.

I saw another resident start to walk toward me so I grabbed them and went back to another nurse to ask what the medication was.

Holy Cow it was Oxycodone at a high dose. Big rule of thumb is never leave medication unattended that's why the nurse carts have locks on them. Any resident could grab it or a visitor's child thinking its candy.

I reported all this to the nurse director and wrote a warning that must be given. Every week I would ask if the warning was done and kept getting excuses. I finally did the warning myself.

Well it didn't stop there. One morning a nurse's aide came to me and said a resident fell on Sunday and none of the aides could find this nurse anywhere. Even after continual pages.

One aide went outside the building to see if the nurse was having a cigarette. Low and behold this nurse was leisurely swinging a golf club out on the lawn.

No radio, nothing. I instructed the Nurse Director to immediately terminate this nurse.

The next day I asked if this was done the Nurse Director tried to appeal this decision saying this was a great nurse. I grabbed the termination letter from this Director and proceeded to end the working relationship with this nurse myself.

Because my ship was sinking fast due to poor sub management, I had to eventually let this Director go as well. That was the second Director I terminated.

I hired a new Director of Nursing who was extremely compassionate, fair, hands-on and great at coaching. A truly hands-on leader who gets right in the trenches and works the hours with their troops.

After this person started we later discovered that previous medical records were not accurate, nurse orders were not placed, favoritism was prevalent, etc. So this new Nurse Director had a huge objective to clean all of this up and get her staff where they needed to be. She did a fantastic job.

The third one was the Dining Director. She was an extremely warm and friendly gal, but she let so much slide when it comes to

State regulated processes such as temping the food, properly labeling open containers, maintaining records, allowing staff to enter without hair nets, etc.

All her food was as if we were incarcerated. Soft meats, potatoes, vegetables and pie. This hardly ever changed. The residents continually complained of getting "mush" all the time. And the budgets were always overspent by month's end all the time.

I tried working with her, but she kept saying she knows what the residents like. Finally after catching her in several noncompliant acts and continually being off budget, I pulled her in my office and placed her on a plan of improvement. This ticked her off and she tearfully gave me her two weeks' notice.

Stuff like that hurts because we invest so much time getting our staff where they need to be. We have a personal investment in them as well as a professional one.

I hired another gal that had extensive experience, but within two weeks she had alienated her whole staff. She would talk a lot about technical compliances and write long letters and leave them under my door about things she was doing to improve the place.

Strangely she started to write up her staff for untrue situations for minor discussions. I later found out she told another manager she wanted to get rid of all the staff and replace them with people from her previous job.

I confronted her with this information and had open discussions with the staff she had written up. This was a lot of unnecessary work folks.

Three of the four write ups were unfounded and I retracted them. I mean this gal had "volumes" of documentation right down to taking to long for a bathroom break to being dinged for faded clothing.

I had a few more discussions with the new Dining Director and finally decided that she wasn't going to work out either.

We decided to pursue a professional Chef this time and interviewed several. There was this one young man who was so cocky and confident that I just had to hire him.

I knew that after working here a month or two his demeanor would change. He was such a proud fella always wanting to prove to me his abilities. His cache of kitchen utensils were not to be touched by anyone and I mean ANYONE!

I thought he came across overly confident and somewhat arrogant, but doggone if I didn't like him. He absorbed all the State compliance training and maintained all that in his department.

He rearranged the kitchen to look like a professional kitchen. This guy was on top of things and very proud of his food preparations. The staff got along with him beautifully. The residents were amazed and extremely happy.

I had to terminate three directors and gut some additional staff that were not in line with our mission and vision. It took me a year to get the staff and new directors in place. Pretty soon the ship was sailing beautifully.

picking a darn good team!

Everyone was doing what they should be doing and compassionate about it. And....I finally was able to take some weekends off. Imagine that! It was all coming together. Something I will always be proud of through my coaching and leadership.

Oh darn…..I knew it was too good to be true….

After two years my husband started to hint that things were not going well with the company he worked for. He liked his job and the staff he worked with but if there's any instability with a company he is the kind of guy who has to work for a company more secure.

I keep telling him that no job or company is truly secure, but this particular company was losing a million a month so I agreed with his decision and started to send his resume out within five nearby States that we were familiar with in the Midwest.

He had several interviews and some very close to offers, but none panned out. He started to get depressed. He does that a lot. It takes everything in my power to keep his momentum up. Try keeping the house clean, building my husband and staff up. No time for "Calgon take me away."

Then I sent his resume to a headhunter for an Engineering Management opportunity in a Northern State. They liked his phone interview and flew him over for a live interview. Two days later they offered him the job and the stress started all over again with planning a move.

I thought of staying and have him fly back since we practically owned our home and my job was going very well by now…but we eventually concluded that we couldn't be apart as we were getting older and just didn't want to spend the extra monies having to live apart.

Chapter XVII

I tearfully told my Operations Manager I was leaving with a good 45 day advance notice. She was devastated and so was I. We spoke to quite a few men and women to take my place and finally settled on a gal that the Operations Manager used to work with. She was smart, organized and very computer savvy. It really gets sad in a minute though.

On my replacements first day, while I was training her on our software programs I was surprised to see our Corporate Human Resources and Regional Operations Manager show up that morning.

What a nice surprise! They had to have flown in on the corporate private jet. I saw a letter in one of their hands and by looking at their faces I could tell this wasn't a visit with good intentions.

Sure enough my regional supervisor drives up and walks in. They asked to meet her privately and I told them they could use my office as I needed to attend the Resident Counsel meeting. So my new replacement and I walked upstairs to the meeting.

When we got back they told me they fired our regional supervisor. Are you kidding me?! She had been there over 6 years! I didn't know how to react at all.

Great timing for my replacement's first day and also knowing that this same boss referred her for the job-how awful this was feeling. All our eyes bugged out. None of us knew why she was terminated or anything. Nothing was explained.

Like I said, you just never know when something is going to happen or what direction it will be. Nothing shocks me anymore, but I could see this was very awkward for the new Director's first day.

By then it was late afternoon and it was a good time to take the new Director out for a lunch just to try to regain some sense of it.

All we talked about was speculation on why they let her go. I finally told her that this is in no way a reflection on her at all and that she needs to remain confident in her abilities. Something like this had to be in the works for a long time.

So many questions, we couldn't even call this person as they confiscated her company cell phone. We had to wait until our day ended.

Thinking back about a year later I had an inkling it was over a series of subordinate conflicts between my supervisor and the other executive directors.

I know this as every time we all met at meetings or training that's all they did was complain about her. I had my own problems but was able to work them out to the point where we became extremely close friends and peers.

I finally got ahold of my supervisor a couple of days later (I didn't want to bother her during this uncomfortable time). But I wanted her to know I supported her.

I later found out that the President never liked her and sure enough the other Directors were constantly complaining about her which most likely had a probable impact on the decision for her eventual termination.

She's a tough cookie and we've had our bouts at times, but we would meet and openly discuss our issues and somehow were able to work it all out by being up front with each other. Our relationship blossomed into a great partnership. She had to be hard to get everyone where they needed to be. I respected that.

Well by now my husband already found temporary housing and moved to his new job. I had to complete unfinished business so I stayed behind a couple of months. I flew up a few times to look at homes with a realtor and go to a couple of job interviews.

Well I left and moved north but kept in contact with several previous workers and residents there. About 6 months later my previous supervisor called me to tell me that one of the corporate Marketing Managers committed suicide. She just got married and promoted to Regional Marketing Manager. I also know she just had a new home built.

A suicide note was discovered and a lot of it was everyday pressures. Sometimes I think there was just a bit too much pressure on people at the home front and workplace. It's hard to balance all of that.

It makes you wonder as those things just don't happen. It is the second time I've experience an employee suicide and no matter what, you just don't get used to it. Shocking every darn time!

I wish I had an opportunity with both to try and talk them out of it. To show them there is so much more to live for. Sunshine, green grass, flowers, other people worse off than them and family. But alas, sometimes we have no control over this. They just can't overcome their deep depression.

During the relocation process my husband and I spent countless hours with a realtor seeing over 30 homes and none were to our liking. This realtor just didn't listen to what we were saying and randomly showed us homes. Some were horribly dirty or damaged and we are a couple with no time for renovation.

One day while surfing the net, I had asked my husband to check out a home I saw online and while he was doing that he passed a very nice home with a "For Sale by Owner" sign on it.

We checked it out and it was absolutely perfect for us. Fairly new with a 3-car garage. Fenced in yard for our killer Chihuahua. A great neighborhood. Close to major cities and yet still quaint. What more could we want?

Now you know me, I don't let grass grow under my feet so I had to find Another Great Career Adventure (echo, echo, echo). I diligently sent out my resumes to anything that was remotely related in the Human Resources field. Surprisingly, I had quite a few interviews, some in healthcare, some in manufacturing.

I finally accepted one in manufacturing. My first week I flew to the corporate headquarters to meet everyone and learn of my job duties. While I was flying over, two of the other interviews I had the same time offered me a job as well. One paying quite a bit more. DARN!

I hated to tell them I had already accepted something elsewhere. Once I commit, I don't turn back. I'm dedicated that way and sometimes that's not always good. Timing is everything. But my integrity of a commitment has always superseded anything else.

Besides, it's a very good Company that has been around for years. It needs some TLC with structure, process improvements, communication and training, but the higher ups recognize this and are making changes accordingly.

Anyway my first week was certainly interesting. I ended up flying to the corporate offices in another state for some preliminary training.

This is so weird (really?), but on my second day we were in a conference meeting with the accounting and HR departments and as we were discussing ideas all of a sudden a fight broke out between the payroll manager and corporate human resources manager. Whoa!

I mean an all-out yelling match. I just couldn't believe this! What?! I mean Whaa-a-a-a-a-a-t?!

During that week I would observe the staff around this HR Manager and none were overly polite to her. I couldn't figure it out as she was very polite and professional to me. Oh well, it wasn't my business as my focus was learning and performing my new job at one of the off sites.

I have to admit that I had some frustrations working under this corporate HR manager, but after a year things got a lot better.

We are just two different personalities. This manager was extremely well educated with HR Law and that was such a benefit with several state facilities.

I respected this manager's knowledge, it was just the way this person handled things. Some subjects went on and on and on when they could have been resolved quickly causing less aggravation and pain.

And this person came from a very different work environment and when you start a new job you tend to go at it feverishly with a "positive" optimistic view and then learn of other's personalities and mold around that.

There were times where I was advised against how I handled some things, but I haven't changed my demeanor in 25 years so I wasn't about to now.

Eventually we were told this person and their assistant was no longer with the company. It was not a comfortable situation for any of left in the HR Department as we knew nothing (maybe that's a good thing), but the new manager was a jovial and respectful person so it all works out.

Again, my philosophy is respecting each and every one and handling their issues as if they were the President of the company even when they do wrong there's a way to handle it with respect.

In the short time that I've been here a lot has improved with over 39% in teamwork, retention, attendance and job knowledge. The company was investing in their managers with new training, better equipment and more communications. I know they want this all to come together and be successful just by what they are doing with all this.

Finally working for a professional growing company. About damn time folks! Yes we still need to work on a lot of things, but it's all good.

It's the usual HR stuff here and you can't plan anything as each day has unexpected hurdles. I'm okay with that and actually thrive on those types of environments.

Chapter XVIII

So we've discussed all kinds of management styles and personalities. In a recap below are the most common management personalities.

1. The best is one who gets right in the trenches with their staff, always available at a moment's notice (24/7), maintains a professional demeanor, handles a crisis calmly, handles the work themselves when needed, and respects every person they are in contact with.

2. Then you have the stern, right to the point manager who doesn't want to spend too much time with individual needs. Cuts to the chase. Doesn't know any staff names after being there a couple of years. Stays in their office all day long with the door shut.

3. Then you have the lazy, always delegates all their work, comes in late, leaves early and blames other departments when things don't go right.

4. Sometimes those are the ones always trying to impress the Presidents or VP's of companies. They don't embrace their own team department. They answer all questions politically correct meaning you really don't get a direct answer.

5. Then you have the controlling, demanding or "I'm the top dog" mentality that always enforces fear in others" to get

them to do their bidding. Or is abrupt when responding to you.

6. And lastly you have the psycho who reacts to everything before engaging the brain. They freak out over any problem. They make a little bump into a mountain. They don't look at all the facts when making decisions. They don't take responsibility.

They ridicule other manager's sometimes in front of others and absolutely know they are always right. Those are the ones who you will never forget working with – **EVER!**

If you are a manager who doesn't embrace their team, you are going to fail. You have to gain respect or no one will work for or with you. There will never be any direction so they'll all do it how they think it should be done. This then causes a breakdown because we're all doing it differently.

How would that be in your home life? Think about it. You get a dog or have a baby, then you don't spend any time with it. Eventually the distance gap grows and grows. The dog or child eventually runs away or doesn't respond to you anymore??

You distrust or lack of trust because you don't know how that person reacts. You know absolutely nothing about that person at all. But then little things start to happen.

Communications have been horrible. Again, no one talks to each other. It's all done by email or phone messaging. My husband said the other day that an engineer was emailing him back and forth.

The emails started to get distorted and off track so my husband just stepped 6 feet to his left and bent over to this engineer and said, "I'm right here Bob, talk to me." WHAT?! This guy was in the same room with him and never talked to him? What are we becoming?

Texting is another bear! I have so many staff texting while working. Yes ma'am, I'm concentrating on my work 100% (sort of).

We have managers giving directives...we follow those directives, then we are later told those instructions were never given or shouldn't have been given in a certain way, that we have to read minds to judge the climate?

Our sense of urgency to complete a task can sometimes get us in a lot of hot water if we do tackle it too fast. We can't read what you really want us to do. But it's our fault, never theirs. I despise it when a manager doesn't take accountability for something they instructed or made a decision on.

Whether it's my fault or not, I always take accountability if it's something that HR had done. It's all of us working together and not just so-and-so over there. You gain a lot more respect when you do that. Just like our kids. I take full responsibility when they didn't know something I should have taught.

Back to management types.

Then there are those that do not maintain confidentiality. I cannot tell how many managers and supervisors have "spilled the beans" so to speak. They live for the attention of knowing something before anyone else does.

It's really bad within the HR Department if you cannot maintain confidential information. You shouldn't be in that role if you are not able to. I know of an HR Generalist who sent out an offer letter to a potential VP and faxed it all over. Naturally I got it first thing in the morning so I called Corporate to tell them what just happened.

An immediate statement went out to pull that off the faxes and shred the information. Well a couple of managers saw it and all hell broke loose when they saw the package deal and offer. We had a lot of explaining to do. Needless to say that gal didn't have a job anymore. BE CAREFUL-USE CAUTION BEFORE HITTING THE "SEND" BUTTON.

Then we had emails going back and forth and people like to hit "Respond to all" without carefully checking the mail forward history. Holy Cow! That can get you in a lot of hot water as well. Delete the message history before you forward.

Here's a big one....

Supervisor's or managers should never be "best friends" with their staff either. You will have more difficulty when the time comes to discuss concerns of that staff member if you are too close with them personally. They also learn an awful lot about you and trust me, its spread all over.

Consistency. Holy cow. I've seen all kinds of issues for not doing it the same for everyone. This is why you get into trouble if you do not remain consistent. No deals...PERIOD! Everyone follows the same rules no matter who they are in the ranks.

I've seen all kinds of different deals in writing (that's a big no-no). We had one I'll tell you about that happened 10 years ago. We evidently put someone on a leave of absence that wasn't FMLA qualified and allowed this person all kinds of benefits that we paid for without putting them on COBRA.

Well evidently this breach in the rule has now cost the company and the employee some serious dollars. This employee remarked that he was promised something and now we were backing out of it.

Our integrity was just eliminated with this action. First, no one discussed it with anyone else in HR. Second, we put it in writing? Man, that's not good. And thirdly we are now backing out of the whole deal? Now it's not just a reflection on the HR department but it's the integrity of the whole darn company.

It was a very nice gesture from the company but it should have been researched in greater depth to ensure we were still compliant.

The sad part is some very nice and hardworking people were blamed unnecessarily for this mishap causing much more hardship that will now always make these employees feel afraid to branch out with ideas.

They were just pushed down a little more, so why try? Again management needs to take accountability and say we all learn from this going forward and keep supporting your team no matter who is at fault.

Negative comments about a company can spread like wildfire in a community. There are so many out there that when I was applying for jobs, people would say, "Oh you don't want to work there, they have an awful reputation."

I can't tell you how many times staff have called me very upset. Their voices would crack and I could tell they were under serious stress over the way a boss made them feel. They were only doing what they were instructed.

All I can say is don't sweat over negative comments from your boss. Believe me that boss has forgotten about it long ago. People who worry, constantly talk about it or beat themselves up are the ones who take great pride in their work. But we're slowly diminishing any confidence left in their abilities.

Even if they do something wrong, there is a way to make them understand it, but it's the talent knowing how to make them feel good in the end. That's also key with disciplines.

They made a mistake, help them understand the whys and then support them to do better. "I have absolute confidence in your abilities and we'll get through this together." "I will support you all the way." How's that for a discipline ending?

Since I am a promoter of people I get emails and calls all the time for support. Even from staff I used to work with from jobs years ago. I'm good at consoling and building character back up. I always apologize to them for their boss's behavior or for the situation that occurred. Even if it's their fault, there is a way to make it right. Shame on all of us.

It's so sad to know that many managers can be just plain mean or rude. No consideration for others. I've seen it both ways. Disrespect to females and males. I had a boss one time make a 59 year old man cry right in front of me. How sad is that?

I get so exhausted working for supervisors that are domineering. Shame on us for not being a solid trusted rock to lean on. I'm fighting a losing battle here folks. Too many like this are out there.

I'm not saying I'm unique, I'm saying I have a passion for my career and know what it actually means. I get so tired though. And I'm so sorry to say this but it's still true that men managers are paid so much more than female managers in the same role.

I truly don't believe this will ever change overall no matter how much time goes by. It's been this way forever. It's natural for us.

Yes, you see female presidents or leaders, but again look at their wages. Still below many times over. Who can break this awful chain? Who? People like me-those with a voice. You bring out the data enough, then it might change (there's my optimism again-dang!). We'd better not go into this one.

The folks that would bend over backwards to make sure all your concerns, ideas, suggestions, and many times personal issues are dealt with expeditiously. To truly and genuinely care. Feel good when you go home know you made an impact on staff at work. I've worked with tons of people like that too.

I fear that I might not stay at my current job. Especially since I've written this book. Ah-h, freedom of speech will get you where you need to be, ~~promoted~~, **fired**-yah that's the one!

My husband tells me to just do my best when I get frustrated. So much going on internally. A lot of departmental changes, reorganizing without any pre-discussion. Always kind of "out-of-way" responses as to why the reorganization.

Maybe middle management isn't supposed to know anything and I might be jumping to conclusions. Jumping to conclusions is due to lack of communication. I had one manager over 13 years ago publicly post everyone's wages and questions on an employee board. ANY QUESTION was posted with a response.

There was no confusion at this place! No rumors, nothing that would take up an HR person's time. It was run like a tight ship.

If you have an HR department that never hears from their leader, never communicates with staff, substantial hires suddenly appear without us knowing and other departments are hush-hush around you, then it doesn't take anyone much to figure out that you ultimately fear being a part of the immediate plan and not the future.

Luckily this was recognized and now a lot of company's hold weekly meetings to go over EVERYTHING. It has resolved a lot of issues going forward.

Now here's a pet peeve of mine. This happened about 8 years ago. When I came to work on a Monday there was a new engineer waiting for me. Gee, I wasn't told we were hiring, who put the ad in? What kind of engineer is he? Who interviewed him?

Where's the offer letter, did anyone do a background check or pre-employment physical? Huh? What am I? Nothing? Yet you want me to orientate him? Gee, sure didn't consider my schedule either now did yah?

Being out of the loop, especially in HR, suspicions develop and are an awful feeling. I have been through the ringer many times over (really?) and have too much dignity and integrity to let a company or anyone take me down anymore.

For years I've heard so many staff say to me that they are indispensable. That no one can do what they do or this company will fail if they let ME go! If I leave 30 others will follow. Are you kidding me? They're not going to follow you!

It's happened so many times in my career to me or others that you just can't say that anymore. YOU ARE REPLACABLE-Period! And let the others go. If they don't want to be here, then we don't want them here.

They don't like people stirring the pot. I don't stir anything anymore, I do my best to resolve things and maintain confidentiality. It's too much work otherwise.

I have expressed some concerns to the higher ups many times and they know that I am not afraid to say something if it's going to affect others. I have no fears or complexes anymore. People will do whatever and nothing surprises me anymore.

Every Plant Manager and supervisor I've worked with gets along with me great. Not many HR leaders in the same department though. We all think we know how to do it better. There tends to be some unhealthy competition when you have several HR people in the same company.

Here's what I've developed at my previous job and received an award for. Or they state they are going to get their GPHR next week or they have a Masters in blah-blah-blah. Who cares? Don't impress me with your certificates. Can you do the job is the question to ask.

Shame on us for instilling fear in our staff to the point we have to justify our position. How dare we do that! We all put our pants on the same way, get over that overbearing behavior and come down to earth and humble yourself.

Chapter XIX

Brings me to my dad who was a high executive for a famous company back home. My dad only had a 7th grade education, but he made several patents and inventions that the company made millions on. One of his inventions is used today and in all grocery or department stores. I'm very proud of that.

Back then you could go right to the top just on your abilities. It didn't take a BA or MA or PHD to get there. But eventually on his 35th year with that company they reorganized and ousted him out over a degreed young engineer. He did get a sizable severance package, but he was only 53 and wasn't ready to retire.

I remember him telling me that when a new young engineer would come on board he would escort them in the direction of the executive lounge. The name plate on the door was so fancy so anyone would assume that wasn't the executive lounge. As dad would walk away, the new engineer would go inside. Yup, you guessed it...it was the broom closet!

He had to get back somehow but in a nice way. Luckily my dad was a previous pilot and got a job in a Southern State flying helicopters spraying for mosquitos and capturing them to test for disease. He did that until he was 67 and decided it was time to retire. Talk about an exciting job! There's always hope.

So where will I go from here? I'm now in my 60's. No degree, but 27 years in HR or Business Management. Got my PHR and SHRM-CP.

I serve as Board of Director on two different boards. I've counseled adults at local colleges on how to get back into the workforce. I've done seminars on effective leadership. I founded a new HR and Business group with 27 members. I am President of my own career counseling company.

Do I feel accomplished? You betcha I do. I hunger to keep going. I love to learn new things on the computer such as The Cloud, SharePoint and other software.

Do I have a chance in this "degreed world?" Sure I do. Remember we have a Governor who doesn't have a degree, the founders of many famous companies did not finish their degrees and are multi-billionaires. Degrees are great! But more and more I believe it's leaning towards skills, personality, accomplishments and common sense.

I just heard that Kirk Kerkorian passed away. He was a gigantic business mogul with only an 8th grade education. Man that guy did so much for the world business wise. A true genius.

I'm not knocking degrees, two of my stepchildren have great degrees, but they also have tons of added skills that will take them very far in this world. It was just not a course for me to follow back then. I was having too much damn fun as you read above!

I've had numerous interviews so a lot of companies that look at both venues. Experience now seems to equal the educational portion as some of the ads say, "Bachelor's or 10 years' experience in lieu of or a combination of education and experience." You see those ads more and more now because we are slowly slacking on skilled labor.

We are having such a hard time finding skilled personnel. I was at a recent job fair and this manager drove 5 hours to the job fair looking for skilled mechanics. He said they had depleted through everyone in his territory.

I would talk to headhunters and staffing agencies. They complain that no one is coming in and registering for work. Jobs are now aplenty everywhere. But finding a "skilled" mechanic or office person is scarce. It's an employee's world out there. We can pick and choose without fear of not eventually being selected.

I'll go to the jobs and stand strong knowing that I will be an effective person there. I've never not felt like an accomplished professional. I've gone a long way in my career and have a feeling it will just keep improving.

It's obvious how fast things are changing in this world. The "X" generation is now in their mid-thirties. I see a lot of reactionary people from that and not those who take a look at the whole picture, get all the facts and weigh the outcomes before *reacting*.

It's gotten us in a whole lot of hot water when we don't take a step back and view the information from all sides. I actually see it within our government and then later they realize it could have been handled better. We need to SLOW DOWN just a bit. Do it right the first time and not over and over.

If you would just walk away from it and go back either later on or the next day, you will see a much different perspective of the same information. That's what I preach with emails. Type your response then get up and walk away. Get a water or coffee. Come back and read it again. You'll be surprised and often times thankful you didn't hit the "send" button before.

We are becoming a "You owe me" mentality. There is no employment exchange anymore. It's an employee's world not an employer's. With all these continual law changes we are losing control of what we can say or do in this business world. Laws are now being formulated and passed by the minute it seems. Makes your head swell with all the new rules.

With such limitations, we tend to sidestep many procedures to get where we need to be but that always comes back negative eventually.

We still have older companies who do not want to change or give up their structure. These types of companies conflict heavily in the modern world and with the younger generation of thinking.

There's no more mental calculating as we have programs to do that for us now. A hard worker isn't what it used to be. It's wrenching, digging, developing a program or process using your damn head for once instead of a computer or calculator.

We have fast food instead of home cooked meals. Too many times I see mom come home and dad leaves for work. No one sits down at the dinner table anymore. No one plays ball with their kids. Buy them a new toy every month, that's keep them busy! What?

I visit some of our younger workers in the lunchroom and their priorities in life are so immediate and different. Nothing for the future. What for? We're young and indestructible. Why should I save now? I've got time.

We're not old like you. (Their talking to me folks). I try to think if I was that way and I can honestly say no. I had a nice savings, big dreams of owning a home, car and growing into a great career at a very young age. I focused on those goals. Back then having a nest egg and a home was the American dream.

I still see so many that just "want a job" to buy more iPads, cellular phones, remote controlled recreation toys, etc. and etc. I see a huge complacent side with our existing and new employees.

At all ages now. So many sad stories of obvious misuse of the workers compensation. So many that I've experienced-shame on you! But we cannot do anything about that because there are laws to protect them.

We live in a very young neighborhood. In fact, I think my husband and I are the oldest people there. Nothing but 25-40 year old couples with little ones everywhere. Some parents are outside with the kids all the time and others are just sitting around texting while the kids are begging for attention.

Here's the kicker folks. I'm more worried about our future due to us being so nonchalant. Our quality control is out the door. You read about it every single day.

Look at some of the products that have been recalled because we did not do our due diligence with researching it fully before selling it to the public. Don't you think our credibility is declining?

There are so many things that break down, the quality of buildings are nowhere near the old construction days, we always find out after a tragedy that we have to change something. WE ARE NOT THINKING AHEAD!

From breaches in airport security to computer hacking to identity theft on a huge scale. Continual oil leaks in the oceans, cruise ship disasters, buildings collapsing, trains colliding, food and equipment recalls. We have become Super Complacent BIG TIME!

Once a tragedy happens **then** and only then do we engage into action and try to fix it. There is no preventative processes or proactive future thinking of "what ifs" to avoid it in the first place. We add to the confusion by forming large committees that take months to handle this.

We are slowly and methodically losing it. Others capitalize on our failures including foreign fright tactics. Others exploit it. Others forget it all together. Think about it….after a while we don't hear anything more about it.

Now the government is controlling our lives. Think about it. They control our health care choices, they regulate our taxes; they now don't allow certain clothing to be worn in public.

They remove certain books out of libraries, our historical flags and currency are being changed, and we can't say prayers in public and on and on. Hey, maybe this book won't be on the shelves either. It is opinionated yah know. What does that sound like to you? You baby boomers know the answer to that one.

Oh and we can no longer spank our children. THIS is why we have school and mall killings and other random acts that children do to become famous. That's because we didn't have time for them when they were young. Disciplining isn't because you are mean, it's because you love them.

I'm sad I'm aging but kind of glad I'm where I'm at in my life. I'm not sure if I want to see how all this turns out.

I can only hope that some of our younger leaders get a grasp on all this and bring us back to where it is safe to walk in your neighborhood, okay to drive down the road without getting in a crash from a texting driver, not worrying over all the bad food recalls or our melting glaciers.

Alas, we are getting more and more paranoid, controlling and demanding. Everything in this world is being scrutinized. I wish I could go back to when you saw the great shows like, Lucy and Desi, Bewitched, Gunsmoke, the Dean Martin Show and so on. When life was so much better. You could joke over just about anything and morals were intact. Life was good then.

Chapter XX

There is so much out there that needs fixing. It's endless…..fixing it with sensibility would be a great outcome indeed.

I will end this book and put the gun away as that's not a solution to anything. Oh shit! God forbid now I'll have someone protesting my gun comments throughout this book. It's just a joke folks. It is the name of my book after all and I'm going to leave it in there. Nah-nah-nah!

YOUR
FIRST AMENDMENT
NEEDS
YOU

Although many times it seemed appropriate in my past job stresses-maybe I should have switched to a squirt gun. At least I would get refreshed every time. Oh-h-h-h and there were so many times.

I will now give you my thoughts on what makes a great HR person or just any type of manager nowadays. I know I started this book with my philosophy of great management and will reiterate some strong points.

You can never get enough of this stuff.

My take on a Strong Human Resources Department or any Management Personnel

I have some rules that I abide by….

1) You can't fix everything
2) At all times, be respectful
3) Don't take sides (get all the facts first)
4) Don't sweat the small stuff
5) You make a commitment-you had better keep it
6) Leave it at the office
7) Take five (it helps to break away even for 5 minutes)

We also have a tendency to discuss our day with our spouse's when we get home from work and that just fuels the fire. You don't know if they've also had a bad day so it just compiles on top and also sets the tone for the evening.

They've worked hard all day and do not deserve to listen to it. Besides, the next day always gives you a fresher perspective of how to view or handle something. Or load the damn gun!

Now as you've read my episodes in Human Resources you are probably thinking this just can't happen to someone all the time.

But I've met other Human Resources professionals and they also have some very odd situations or controlling bosses as well. Maybe not so flamboyant, but really weird at times.

Gosh, I keep getting off track but some of my writings spur another HR memory story.

I have to tell you one I just remembered....when I was having lunch with a best friend. She is also an HR Manager. She worked at a bank. One day she was interviewing a candidate around 4:30 pm.

When it became 5:00 pm she was still in the interview process and her boss came into her office and turned out the lights. I'm chuckling. WTF? How rude is that? You're right in the middle of an interview and the lights go out?

How frickin insane! We went to lunch one day and we sat down and noticed her boss a few tables over. Every few minutes her boss would look at her watch as if timing my friend to see if she exceeds her lunch hour.

Okay this is what we are paying the big bucks for. Managers like this who nothing better to do except be MEAN! Needless to say she had a very controlling boss and left that job for a much better one that she's been at for 10 years now. You see it always works out. But Dang!

I truly believe that often times our personalities and sometimes our upbringing can dictate where we end up in regards to careers. My upbringing wasn't the best, but somehow again it made me focus on being the better person in life.

Most of my successes were based on two things. First and foremost my personality was always a well-rounded type (so is my body-ugh). It baffles me how I came away with that type of characteristic being around so much negativity throughout my life.

And secondly my skills that I acquired throughout the years. I absorbed and I practiced. I gained vast amounts of education on the job and applied it consistently. To this day my organization skills and personality haven't changed for 30 years.

I see a lot of quiet introvert personalities and they don't like stirring anything up. They will just do the everyday duties and never volunteer for extra. I actually have worked with some sorely miserable people. I would walk up to them and ask for something and they would never give you eye contact.

They would mumble a response. Some don't respond at all. There's an employee I say good morning to every day and he never responds back so one morning I did my usual "Good Morning" to him, no response.

So as I'm walking past his office I loudly say, "Well Good Morning to you also K, you are looking quite lovely today." He would just star at me. Did yah get my drift sir? Did it sink in? You need to respond to those who talk to you or it's considered

RUDE!

The extroverts or people who always want to be "out there" feel itchy to get going, explore new things, be the voice of others. They always work on committees and volunteer for extra.

Remember, a career history needs to be treated just like a credit balance. You have to have a good credit history to purchase things, so you also need a good career history to gain good positions.

I've moved around a lot. Probably had 4 jobs in the last 10 years. That may seem like a lot, but some hiring managers don't look at that anymore. They look at what you've done or why you left.

Always put in your accomplishments on a resume as well and make sure it's concrete impacting information. BE HONEST in your resume as it WILL catch up to you.

Never quit on a whim, always have work references and not just personal-that's a huge part of your professional credit history. You have to have previous supervisory references. Always and again I mean always update your resume the minute you start a new career.

Don't wait six months down the road. I've had so many people get laid off or let go and don't have an updated resume. Careers are not going to wait for you…you have to be ready for the moment.

Stay focused on what you really would like to do and what type of environment you want to be in. Research the jobs you are applying to thoroughly. Too many times they will ask you what you know about their company and you can come across highly valuable if you've done your homework.

Dress nicely, professionally, preferably in a suit. If it's a hot summer day, a nice shirt and casual pants or skirt is recommended.

Read between the lines in interviews as it's never enough information even after a couple of meetings. Watch employees when you take a tour of the facility to see body languages that might give you clarity.

Taking on a new profession is a huge investment and you need to be at least 75% sure before you sign the dotted line.

I used to counsel students in high schools on how to gain their first job if they hadn't already. I'd walk in the gymnasium with a frumpy blouse half out of my skirt, a run in my panty hose, my hair all messed up, chewing and popping gum. I'd get some laughs but then I'd ask them if they think I'd be employable.

Then I go behind a curtain and straighten myself out and ask the same question again. Too many applicants do not think their appearance is a factor and it's a HUGE first impression.

Some of my superiors would tell you they viewed me as too soft and nice, not a delegator. But many of my peers and co-workers will tell you just the opposite.

I gave them plenty more responsibility and I just handle things in a calm and respectful manner. If I can't handle a project well, I always ask for help with it. I don't yell and intimidate as many prefer to do.

I've terminated over 500 people in my career and many were upper management. I don't get nervous doing them or rude. It is what it is. I view being bossy or harsh will only gain you that reputation and you will falter eventually.

Most human resources people I've known are always angry or irritated because they have to handle everyone's issues and get them resolved. There's little patience with this job. Shall I tell you about Union HR people? A whole new story there. They complain to me all the time.

I also get very frustrated and want to just walk away. Remember that, because walking away can sometimes give you time to rethink the handling of a subject in a much more professional manner.

Who helps us? Who supports the Human Resources Managers? Upper management should not be the resource of any assistance or backup.

They have their own agendas and dealing with staff is last on their list. They earned that right and that's why we, the sub-management get to do all the fun and crazy stuff.

But if you are an HR Generalist, your boss better damn well be a total support for you and not put everything on your agenda. They should be a "working" leader helping you with many things. That's what makes a great HR department team.

Here's who supports us:

Our comrades we work with daily within our organization such as SHRM or local HR groups and other management peers. Networking is so important these days. All of us have a story to tell and we really wish it was fictional but it never is.

We have to be the ones who always smile, always be available and always a resource to everyone. In some instances 24/7. Of all the crap we take and dole out, don't you ever wonder if how you handled it really mattered? Of course it does. We are the glue for everything.

But we have personal lives too. A lot of times different department managers think they are the only ones asking us for help? They need to realize when you have twelve department managers that they are not the sole attention getter.

But our jobs are tough to measure economically. How do we show the value of an HR department? We have to show it by improved retention, hiring qualified personnel, having less workers compensation and safety claims, more productivity and so on.

One thing that really irks me is when you are handling a situation with an employee and follow through, then go back a week later to ensure it's all working out….but this person fails to tell you weeks later that it's not resolved.

And instead of going back to you or following the chain of command by going to the Corporate HR person, instead they go straight to the President of the company with the issue. I've seen this so many times. Now we are blindsided as we thought we hopped on it right away and fixed things.

Some staff avoid the immediate supervision altogether doing it this way and it's not a wise thing to do. The President naturally contacts me and I now have to become "defensive" and back up everything I did and truly surprised (and pissed) by this action.

But the information given to the President stated nothing had been done. Thank goodness for witnesses in meetings and email documentation, otherwise it's he said she said. I mean this happens a lot folks.

Now I'm taking the yoga approach.

Chapter XXI

As I lean back, stretch and reflect these last 60 years of everything I've experienced I sometimes wonder if I'd be better at other things instead of HR. As I was when I was a Director of a retirement community.

Or when I ran a business office doing so much more than just HR. Nah! I still feel I'm grounded in HR as my core career choice. If they'd just stop making all these damn law changes and upgrades. Geeze, stop already!

Even now the staff and peers from my last 6 jobs still email me asking for advice. That's over 20 years ago. You have to believe that I did such a good job that I had impacted everyone there to this day. Do you know how great it feels to leave a professional legacy behind? I mean think about it.

Maybe it was because we are dealing with people instead of making a product? No, I don't think either is significant because people make the product or do the service. People work hard in both sectors.

I believe I have been truly blessed with the gift of being able to impact others no matter where I work or no matter who I meet on my road through life. Both professionally and personally at work or not at work.

Gosh I will never forget that one of my directors told me after teaching her how to manage herself at work had actually made her a better mom for her child. Say what?!

She also was not contacting her mom a lot and I actually got her to become closer to that relationship too. She even brought her son and mom into work one day and I think she felt proud about that. It felt so good to know that. Those are the things that make me a truly "accomplished person" in life.

Getting Better Day by Day

Chapter XXII

Well…….

I have now taken on a new job elsewhere and yes I am still in Human Resources. This company has been around for years and there was a lot going on internally that I could write about but it's not really crazy stuff, nothing like in my earlier days or worth mentioning.

It's more of a "lack of communication" nature of things and that's pretty normal within cluster organizations. But the chief person running this company has very good intentions and knows the right direction to take, so it's all good here.

Besides I didn't want to write anything bad especially if I still work here. Whoa! Don't burn your bridges folks as it's not worth it even if you quit-leave on good terms. No career is ever perfect, just like a relationship. It's constant work.

But then who knows? Some of those types of companies <u>still do exist out there</u>. I know because I had an interview with one before I got this job. Every statement in that interview was illegal!

Geez, I'm going to go off track again, but that's what this is all about. Getting back on track. Anyway, about this interview. This job was in a bad part of town, you'd walk in and the reception office had bullet proof windows (nice touch).

You ask where the bathrooms are and someone escorts you in. You turn to lock it and notice not one, but THREE dead bolts on the door. I feverishly look around for security cameras. No way am I sitting on that seat folks! There's red stain everywhere, WTF?

When you interview, it's very informal. You could hear a 2-way radio in the background with staff talking back and forth throwing out the "F"-bomb here and there. You go through the entire interview and find out they have no benefits at all. Then they notify you of the wage which is way below what you are wanting for the area. How are they getting people?

When you finished the interview they walked you out holding an attack dog on a leash escorting you back to your car. I also remember as I was walking out I noticed another candidate sitting in the so-called "reception" area with her eyes wide open and bugged out. I could tell she was also thinking to herself, "What the heck am I doing here?" Boy now is when I REALLY need that gun!

You know we always seem to go through so much in life and you have to wonder how we get where we are. I know a couple of younger folks that are always blaming other things and really not taking a look at what they are doing or decisions they are making which is most likely why these things are happening.

I've given them specifics as to the "whys" but they refuse to accept it. I despise it when someone says, "This is happening to me because of the way my parents raised me."

That just isn't so. YOU are in control of YOU. We have the power to change anything. Why fear change? Do you really like where you are right now?

Do I miss that the 70's, 80's and 90's work era? Hell Yes I do! It was so loose then. You actually had Freedom of Speech then. Not anymore. Too many laws for every damn little thing. We've gotten ourselves in such bad situations from other's opinions. I feel it's only going to get worse just from all the crap on the news.

We've taken away so much of our history because it offended someone today. Pretty soon they'll remove the show Bewitched because they drank on television or the Brady Bunch because the parents were divorced.

It's getting so bad now. We are complaining or suing for things that happened over 50 years ago. We are slowly eliminating our heritage and culture originating from that by removing certain flags or president's names on schools because of their way of life back then which again was our <u>historical origination!</u>

Now it's nothing but zombies, blood and guts everywhere. Yeah that's our future heritage. Are you kidding me? Seriously, take a review of the movies that meant something, had a plot, great acting to now. Walking on land moaning and looking like you've been run over by a train! Who doesn't want to have some popcorn watching that shit?

I have to tell you that I am so amazed that I've come this far after everything I've gone through in life. I mean think about it. I've actually only given half of my life story which is bad enough. I consider myself an extremely accomplished professional who has undergone a bottomless pit of agony in the personal and professional arena so how did I get here?

I'll tell you how. I have so much hope and love for myself and others that it kept me from becoming a drug addict or alcoholic. I'm actually surprised that I never became either somewhere along the lines. I am a firm believer it's how much you care about yourself and also proving to others that you are better than this. Many have gone through similar personal tragedies such as mine and never made it.

I constantly get staff in my office who say, "You have no idea." Well...actually yes I do in fact. So many have told me even today that my personality needs to be harsher or sterner. I'm never going to make it to the top in the HR professional world because I'm compassionate, honest and not a Delegator.

I beg to differ. I always **terminate with a smile!**

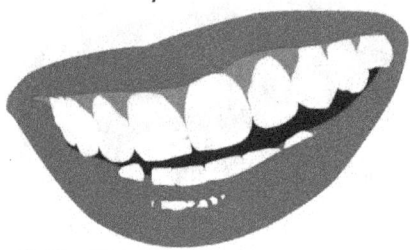

If you are harsh, curt and you delegate every piece of your work, then YOU are not going to make it in the HR profession….Period! You need to know how to do it before you can give it to someone else. What good does it do to have a reputation of a B@#ch? Is it worth it?

Or is it better to know how many people you helped today.

I had an annual review by a previous supervisor who actually wrote in my review that because I wasn't a "harder" person like them, that I was going to get a bad mark for that on every category. Are you kidding me?

Because I don't have your b@#ch personality, I'm being docked? What a load of crap! Worst evaluation I've ever encountered in my career and it did not sit well with me. To me it only made my supervisor look stupid.

This person had input too much of our personal working relationship in this review and it should have been more on what was accomplished. You can't do last minute changes on a review based on things that just happened or heard. It has to be over the whole year. But they do it and I've seen them do it.

Any professional needs to show that they will support others and help out when it's appropriate.

So…..more adventures are out there and I'll bet they find me somehow. You know me, I'm a magnet for crazy. Otherwise there wouldn't be anything else to write about.

H-m-m-m-m-m-m-m…. (I'm pondering now)

Well maybe the next one will even be even more of a doozy tale.

Nah….I'm at a point where I'm not in the doozy era anymore. Too many rules. **Oh Really?**

But wait!

I know what I'll do……I'll write even more about my previous love life. How many? Give me a moment….I'm counting on my fingers and toes….I need more fingers (are you kidding me?) No, unfortunately there are many to write about that could possibly make you pee your pants. Wait…that was me one time! What?

NOW THAT'S A WHOLE NEW FREAK SHOW!

See you on the rebound!

Lady K

www.ingramcontent.com/pod-product-compliance
Lightning Source LLC
Chambersburg PA
CBHW071652090426
42738CB00009B/1497